AF812713

人生与財富

雁

Financial Flow

THE ART OF FULFILLING LIFE AND OPTIMIZING WEALTH

Violetta Sit Terpeluk
MBA, CFP®, CEPA®

Violetta Sit Terpeluk -- 1st ed. Chief Editor, Shannon Buritz

ISBN: 978-1-954757-62-2

To my family — Paul, Ivan, and Lesya — my greatest sources of love and motivation. And to our clients and team — your trust is a privilege, and your journey an inspiration.

Contents

Introduction

For many retirees, business owners, and successful professionals, the ideal outcome is a life defined by freedom. Imagine having the freedom of time—the ability to do what you want, when you want, with the people who matter most. Freedom of money means you have the financial resources to fuel your goals and dreams, eliminating the stress of not having enough and instead focusing on how your wealth can align with the life you envision. Not every dream requires money, but having the financial flexibility to pursue your passions opens the door to a more intentional, fulfilling life.

Freedom of relationship is equally transformative as you let go of toxic relationships and surround yourself with people who uplift and inspire you. Whether it's putting distance between difficult clients, coworkers, or even friends who no longer align with your values, this freedom allows you to create a circle of relationships built on mutual respect and positivity. Life is too short to spend time with people who drain your energy.

Finally, freedom of purpose is living a life in alignment with what truly matters to you. Too many people spend their days doing work that doesn't inspire them, often sacrificing their passions to meet financial obligations. Freedom of purpose is the opposite—it's waking up daily with a deep sense of fulfillment, knowing that what you're doing matters to your family, community, or even the world at large.

In Japan, there's a concept called *ikigai*, which translates to "reason for being." It's the intersection of doing what you love, excelling at what you do, delivering value by solving the world's problems, and being rewarded for it—financially or otherwise. To achieve this kind of life, you must focus not only on the essentials—having food on the table and a roof over your head—but also on creating a lifestyle that brings joy and satisfaction. You must prepare for life's inevitable surprises, plan for the unexpected, and ensure your future is secure no matter what comes your way. Too often, people avoid thinking about these challenges. They don't want to discuss long-term care, the possibility of living longer than expected, or even the legacy they'll leave behind. But avoiding these conversations doesn't make the challenges go away—it only leaves you less prepared.

You might wonder why you haven't already achieved your desired freedom and fulfillment. Many people don't have an accurate sense of where they are right now. How can you map the way if you start a journey knowing your destination but not your starting point? It's the same with financial and life planning. Without an honest assessment of your current reality, charting a meaningful path forward is impossible. This lack of clarity can leave people wandering and unsure of how to make real progress.

You also need to know where you want to go. Many people don't dream big enough; they settle for a vague idea of the future rather than creating a bold, inspiring vision. It's like saying you want to travel but have no idea which city, country, or continent you'd like to visit. If you don't know where you're heading, staying where you are is easy.

Even when you know where you are and where you'd like to go, the next hurdle is finding the most efficient and effective way to get there. People often lack the tools, knowledge, or guidance to create a direct route to their goals. Worse still, they don't anticipate or prepare for the inevitable obstacles that will arise. Life isn't a straight path, and challenges will come up—unexpected expenses, market shifts, health issues, or family needs. Preparing for these potential disruptions is critical, yet most people overlook it.

Sometimes, I use a metaphor to explain this. Imagine traveling from Sacramento to Lake Tahoe, but instead of heading directly there, your route takes you to San Francisco, then across the Pacific Ocean to Hong Kong. You're way off course, and without a strong sense of where you are or where you're going, you have no way to choose the right vehicle, let alone plan for any turbulence along the way.

I've noticed two camps of people from my conversations over the years. There are those who believe everything will be fine as long as life stays predictable. They feel mostly secure but carry a nagging sense that something is missing. They can't quite put their finger on it, but they know there's an uncertainty they haven't addressed—risks they can't identify, quantify, or plan for. This unease keeps them from feeling fully confident about their future.

In the second camp are those who think they're completely fine and don't need help. They resist facing reality and avoid the hard conversations about what could go wrong. They convince themselves that everything will work out, often based on an incomplete or inaccurate picture of their current situation. But this false sense of security can be dangerous, leaving them unprepared for unexpected events that could derail their plans.

In both cases, the result is the same: they remain stuck. My mission is to help people break free from these patterns—to give them the tools and confidence to understand where they are, define where they want to go, and navigate the journey with clarity and resilience.

When it comes to finances, fear can be a paralyzing force. In your quest to make smart financial decisions, you can find yourself drowning in advice, data, and strategies. Instead of feeling empowered, you freeze, unsure of which path to take. This is especially true when it comes to working with financial professionals. Many worry they'll invest money into financial planning but won't see a meaningful return on investment. After all, financial planning is intangible—it's not a physical product you can hold in your hands—and that makes it harder for people to feel confident in what they're paying for.

Another fear is rooted in trust. Even those who feel financially secure often hesitate to hire a professional because they fear making the wrong choice. They worry about trusting someone who may not have their best interests at heart or could leave them in a worse position than where they started. There's an underlying belief that financial advisors are simply out to sell them something they don't need. They worry about being offered cookie-cutter solutions—a one-size-fits-all product that isn't tailored to their unique situation. This suspicion often comes from bad experiences or the perception that advisors are more interested in their business development than genuinely helping clients.

When asked who or what they believe is blocking their success, many investors often point to external forces—the financial industry, taxes, Wall Street, or even specific products like annuities or life insurance. Some even view financial advisors as the enemy, believing advisors are just another cog in the machine selling unnecessary products. The real enemy isn't the market, government, or certain players in the financial industry. The real enemy is often the investor's behavior. Behavioral finance research shows that most investment outcomes—up to nearly 90%—are driven by the investor's own behavior, not the performance of the market. Emotional decisions, lack of planning, and failure to act can have a far greater impact on financial outcomes than any external factor.

Addressing these issues starts with honesty, education, and

accurate thinking. By helping you understand where you stand and what's possible for your future, we can move past the paralysis caused by fear and mistrust. Together, we can tackle the internal and external obstacles and chart a course toward true financial freedom.

In the following pages, you'll explore questions like:

- *What does a fulfilling life mean to me beyond numbers and achievements?*
- *How can I define financial freedom in a way that aligns with my deepest values?*
- *Where am I right now, and what truths have I been avoiding?*
- *Which values should guide my decisions when life feels uncertain?*
- *How can I ensure my money supports the life I truly want to live?*
- *When is it time to reach out for guidance and partnership?*
- *What shifts in mindset and habits will help me move forward with clarity and purpose?*

With over two decades of experience in financial life planning, I've dedicated my career to guiding individuals like you through some of life's most important transitions. Our practice's specialties include retirement planning, distribution strategies, multigenerational legacy planning, and business exit strategies. We've worked hand-in-hand with many individuals and families, helping them retire and, most importantly, navigate retirement with confidence and purpose. Individual financial planners may do things differently; however, I will focus on my processes and practices for this book.

My FLOW system, *Fulfilling Life, Optimizing Wealth*—guides our practice's work. It's a methodology I've developed through years of experience, designed to address the unique challenges and opportunities that come with planning for the future. In FLOW, you're living your life to the fullest, embracing all the freedoms that matter. That's the ultimate goal—leading a life so rich in meaning and joy that you wouldn't change a thing.

Optimizing wealth plays a key role in providing the financial resources to support a fulfilling life. I call this the "head return"—tangible, measurable outcomes. You see the numbers in your accounts, know you have the right insurance policies, and feel prepared for the future. But another piece is just as important, if not more so: the "heart return." This is the peace and joy that comes from knowing you're living your best life. It's the sense of connection with the people you love, the impact you're making in the world, and the deep satisfaction that comes from living in alignment with your values.

Achieving that outcome requires more than good intentions—it necessitates a thoughtful, personalized approach. The INDIGO Journey offers just that: a structured yet flexible process that blends the art and science of financial decision-making.

Each step of the INDIGO Journey addresses a key area that influences long-term confidence and alignment:

- **I** – *Individualized Path*: Designing a plan as unique as you are
- **N** – *Natural Rhythm*: Pacing your journey to match life's seasons
- **D** – *De-Risking*: Protecting what you've built
- **I** – *Implementation Accountability*: Turning insight into sustained action
- **G** – *Goal-Based Investing*: Aligning your investments with what matters most
- **O** – *Orchestration of Your Professional Team*: Coordinating advice and execution

These six steps form the backbone of this book—each chapter explores one stage of the INDIGO Journey.

Writing this book is deeply personal for me—it's part of my own fulfilling life. My goal is to touch more lives, even those I may never meet or work with directly. I've had the privilege of guiding numerous individuals through their financial journeys and seeing the good, the bad, and the ugly. I've witnessed the pitfalls that hold people back, the mistakes that could have been avoided, and the untapped potential of dreams left unrealized.

I want you to see the life you're capable of creating and to take bold steps toward it. I want you to understand that a fulfilling life isn't just a dream—it's achievable with the right mindset, tools, and guidance. As you turn the page, I invite you to open your eyes to the possibilities, confront the hurdles, and step into the most complete version of yourself. Together, we'll uncover what it means to live in your FLOW, creating a life where your heart and your head are at peace, and fulfillment and financial freedom become your reality.

- Violetta Sit Terpeluk

PART ONE

FULFILLMENT BEYOND FINANCES (THE "WHY" AND "WHEN")

Chapter ONE

The FLOW Mindset

"You are not successful until you are living in your flow."
- Roger Hamilton

When discussing financial planning, people tend to jump straight into the "what" and the "how." "*What should I invest in?*" "*How can I grow my wealth?*" These are important, but they miss the bigger picture. The real question we should start with is **why.** Why do you even have money? Why do you have those financial goals?

That's where the FLOW mindset comes in. FLOW stands for Fulfilling Life, Optimizing Wealth. It's about putting life first and money second. Before diving into strategies and action plans, you must understand the purpose behind your money. The ultimate "why," in my opinion, is that money exists to enable us to live a fulfilling life.

Money doesn't exist in a vacuum. Yet, so often, we treat it as though it does. People say, "I want my money to grow. I want it to generate income. I want it to do this or that." But they rarely stop to ask themselves why. Why do you want your money to grow? What kind of life do you want to live? If you're unclear about the life you want, how can you make meaningful decisions about money? Once you know the kind of life you want to lead, giving your money a job and a purpose becomes easier.

My approach to financial planning comes from blending Eastern and Western perspectives. I grew up in a Chinese culture that emphasizes a holistic way of thinking—seeing beyond yourself, beyond the now. Then, I moved to the United States, where I received my education and embraced Western financial principles. These principles focus on action, optimization, and ensuring money works efficiently.

The balance between the two is the foundation of the FLOW mindset. On one hand, Fulfilling Life reflects Eastern, holistic, or even feminine energy, dreaming of a life you truly want. On the other hand, Optimizing Wealth brings in the Western, action-oriented, or masculine energy, making sure your money does the best possible job to support that dream. As we move forward, you'll see how this mindset transforms financial planning from stressful and complicated to meaningful and empowering.

After practicing financial planning for over two decades, I started noticing patterns. I've seen clients who have achieved financial success but aren't happy. On the other hand, I've worked with clients who have enough money and are deeply fulfilled. So, I kept asking myself, what's the difference? What separates the happy from the unfulfilled? The answer was that money is aligned with values, goals, and purpose. That's when I realized the need for the FLOW framework.

Traditional financial planning often focuses solely on the numbers. While those are important, they don't tell the whole story.

Financial success doesn't guarantee happiness. That's why FLOW is different—it starts with you.

The FLOW framework asks:

- What life do you want to live?
- What truly fulfills you?
- How can your money support that vision?

When you're in FLOW, everything feels like water flowing effortlessly towards gravity. That's the image I like to use when explaining this concept. Water flows naturally and adapts as it moves. If there's a rock in its path, water flows around it. It's flexible, persistent, and purposeful, and that's exactly how your money should work for you.

Another core idea of FLOW is finding the path of least resistance. It's like stepping into a natural rhythm when your money aligns with your values. Suddenly, financial planning doesn't feel like a chore. That doesn't mean there isn't work involved. FLOW is also about direction and structure. Like water, which flows with gravity yet follows a specific path, the FLOW framework incorporates a process.

Why Growing Wealth Isn't Enough

When I consider why money matters, I can't help but get emotional. Growing wealth for the sake of growing wealth—what's the point? It becomes an empty exercise if you don't understand the purpose behind your money.

Think about it:

- Is your money enabling you to live a good quality of life?
- Is it helping you build generational wealth to support your family for years to come?
- Does it empower you to give back—to donate and make an impact in the world?
- Can you care for loved ones, like elderly parents overseas?

I often refer to Maslow's hierarchy of needs, which illustrates human motivation. At the base are the essentials: food, shelter, and security. As you move up, you see things like connection, self-actualization, and, eventually, self-transcendence.

Money plays a critical role in helping us move through these levels. At the most basic level, it provides for our survival. But as we grow, it becomes an enabler for more—helping us connect with others, realize our potential, and ultimately, make a difference in the world. This is why money doesn't exist in a vacuum. It exists in the context of our goals, values, and the kind of life we want to lead.

The truth is money magnifies who you are. If you're generous, it enables you to give more. If you're family-oriented, it helps you care for loved ones. If a cause drives you, it empowers you to contribute on a bigger scale.

But if you're unhappy and unfulfilled, more money won't change that. I've seen people with significant wealth who are still unhappy. That's why I urge you to dream bigger. Money isn't the goal. It's the tool that enables you to reach your dreams, make an impact, and live a truly fulfilling life.

Addressing Misconceptions with the FLOW Framework

Misconception 1: Jumping Straight into "How"

One of the biggest misconceptions is that people want to dive straight into the "how." They'll ask, "How do I allocate my money? Which professional money manager should I use? Should I buy long-term care insurance? How should I convert my traditional IRA to Roth IRA?" without stepping back and taking a 30,000-foot view of their lives. Start with your why. What do you want out of life? What purpose does your money serve? If you skip this step, you risk focusing on details that may not even fit your bigger picture.

Misconception 2: Money is Just Numbers

Many people believe financial planning is only assets, numbers, and returns. They think, "I don't need to talk about my values, emotions, or beliefs about money." But that's simply not true. I often explain financial planning as a puzzle. You need to step back and look at the entire picture to put the pieces together. If you only focus on one piece—like your net worth or investment returns—you'll never see how everything fits together.

To illustrate:

- Net worth is assets minus liabilities.
- Cash flow is income minus expenses.

If you ignore liabilities and focus only on assets, you're not seeing the whole picture. Financial health requires balance—understanding every puzzle piece and how it works together.

Misconception 3: Life Follows Predictable Rules

Another common myth is that life and finances follow predictable rules, like, "A 7% annual return is enough" or "I can withdraw 3% and be fine." While these rules of thumb might work in ideal circumstances, life is rarely that simple.

I always say, "Hope for the best, but prepare for the worst." Life isn't predictable. You could face illness, unexpected expenses, or even death tomorrow. At the same time, you can't live in fear and think, "What's the point of planning if I could die tomorrow?"

Planning creates direction and adaptability. Just like driving a car, you need to know your destination. Are you headed to the office, Lake Tahoe, or Asia? Sure, obstacles might arise along the way, but having a plan helps you adjust and stay on course.

This is why I emphasize the difference between a plan and planning. A plan implies something fixed, but planning is an ongoing process. Having a plan doesn't mean you'll avoid all obstacles, but it does make you more adaptable and optimistic. With FLOW, you can prepare for the worst while living fully in the moment.

The Key Elements of the FLOW Framework

1. FULFILLING LIFE

The first component of the FLOW framework focuses on understanding what truly matters to you. Before even looking at your money, we dive deep into your life vision, asking questions like:

- What kind of life do you want to live?
- If you were financially secure, would you change anything?

- Imagine you had 5-10 years left to live. What would you change about your life?
- Would you have regrets if your life ended tomorrow?
- Do you feel aligned with your core values and purpose?
- What are the essential elements for you to live a fulfilling life?

This part of the process is intentionally disconnected from money because money is simply a tool—it's not the driver of your fulfillment. Some things that bring you joy and meaning might not even require money, and that's okay.

We explore the 12 facets of your life:

- **Health and Fitness:** Do you take care of your physical health through regular exercise, good nutrition, and adequate rest, allowing you to feel energetic and capable?
- **Intellectual Life:** Do you actively engage your mind through learning, curiosity, and mental challenges that inspire you to grow?
- **Emotional Life:** Do you manage your emotions effectively, maintain a positive outlook, and feel emotionally balanced in your daily life?
- **Spirituality Life:** Do you feel a sense of connection to something greater than yourself, and do you engage in practices that bring you inner peace and meaning?
- **Character:** Do you live in alignment with your values, demonstrating integrity, honesty, and the traits you admire most in yourself?
- **Love and Meaningful Connections:** Do you experience love, trust, and mutual respect in your close connections, whether with a partner or other significant relationships?

- **Family and Close Relationships:** Do you feel connected to your family and closest relationships, and do you nurture these bonds with care and attention?
- **Social Life and Community:** Do you enjoy meaningful relationships with friends and community and feel a sense of connection and belonging?
- **Quality of Life:** Do you feel satisfied with your overall lifestyle, including how you spend your time, the activities you enjoy, and the environment you live in?
- **Life Vision:** Do you have a clear vision for your life, and do you feel you are moving toward goals that are meaningful and inspiring to you?
- **Financial Life:** Do you feel confident about your financial stability, security, and ability to use your resources to support your goals and values?
- **Career or Business:** Do you feel fulfilled by your professional path, whether in your career, business ownership, or other endeavors that bring purpose and meaning?

You'll rate yourself in each area and think about where you want to be in the next three months, five years, or over a lifetime.

2. OPTIMIZING WEALTH

Once we've defined your vision for a fulfilling life, we shift to the second component: Optimizing Wealth. Here, we act as your family's financial planner, ensuring that your finances align with your life goals.

Many advisors jump straight into investments, but we take a more strategic approach:

★ **Cash Flow**

- Are you confident that your steady cash inflows cover your essential needs, discretionary expenses, gifts, and donations? Are you in control of your spending, ensuring that your money flows in the directions that matter most to you?

★ **Net Worth**

- Does your net worth provide you with a sense of stability and confidence for your current life stage? Are your assets aligned with your core values and long-term goals? Does your net worth generate enough income to support your desired lifestyle and future aspirations?

★ **Retirement Management**

- Do you have a comprehensive retirement strategy that adapts as you transition through different stages of life? Whether you're building wealth, generating sustainable income during retirement, or preserving your assets for the future, does your plan give you confidence and peace of mind?

★ **Goal-Oriented Planning**

- Are your major financial goals seamlessly integrated into your overall financial plan according to your life stage and significant events? Whether you're saving for a home, funding education, starting or transitioning a business, or preparing for other key milestones, does your plan provide a clear path to achieving what matters most to you?

- ★ **Risk Management and Insurance Planning**
    - Do you use disciplined methods to identify and mitigate risks that could devastate your financial well-being? Are you thoroughly evaluating and implementing insurance and other protection strategies to safeguard what you've built?
- ★ **Tax Planning and Tax Management**
    - Are you actively working to minimize your tax burden in the short and long term? Do you incorporate tax considerations into your financial decisions to ensure tax efficiency and optimize financial outcomes? Are you making smart, tax-efficient investment decisions?
- ★ **Estate and Legacy Planning**
    - Does your estate plan give you confidence that your wealth will be smoothly transferred to your heirs and the causes you care about? Have you ensured that your legacy aligns with your values and wishes, providing peace of mind for you and your loved ones?
- ★ **Investment Planning and Investment Management**
    - Do you follow a disciplined investment approach that aligns with your life stage, goals, and risk tolerance? Are you equipped with strategies to manage your emotions and avoid impulsive decisions, ensuring your investments support your short-term and long-term financial objectives?

Life is constantly changing—your goals, priorities, and circumstances evolve over time. Maybe you've sold your business, become a widow, remarried, or welcomed grandchildren. Whatever the case, financial life planning is never a one-and-done process. That's why "fulfilling" and "optimizing" are verbs. The FLOW framework is a lifelong quest, revisited and refined to reflect the current phase of your life.

Return on Life

When most people think about financial planning, they focus on return on investment (ROI). But that leads to an important question: What are you investing in? And why? If your money isn't helping you live a better, more fulfilling life, then even the best ROI is meaningless.

That's why I like to add the concept of return on life: put life first and money next. Imagine this: You've accumulated wealth and achieved good returns, but are afraid to use your money. You may be hoarding it or unsure how to spend it in a way that aligns with your values and dreams. You might have a great ROI in that case, but your return on life is near zero.

The purpose of money is to serve your life. It should enable you to maintain or enhance your lifestyle, dream bigger about what's possible, contribute more to the causes and people you care about, and live in alignment with your core values and life purpose. If your money is optimized but you're not fulfilled, you only have ROI. If your money empowers you to live a fulfilling life, that's when you achieve a true return on life.

Consider the FLOW Quadrants, visualized as a 2x2 matrix. One axis represents "Fulfilling Life," ranging from low to high, and the other represents "Optimizing Wealth," also ranging from low to high.

- **Low Optimizing Wealth, Low Fulfilling Life:** This quadrant represents a state where neither financial optimization nor life fulfillment is prioritized. This signifies a need to reassess both areas for a more balanced and rewarding existence.

- **High Optimizing Wealth, Low Fulfilling Life:** You primarily focus on ROI (Return on Investment), potentially neglecting your overall well-being.
- **High Fulfilling Life, Low Optimizing Wealth:** You prioritize ROL (Return on Life), finding fulfillment even without maximizing financial resources.
- **High Optimizing Wealth, High Fulfilling Life:** You achieve both ROI and ROL, the optimal alignment where your financial prosperity and personal fulfillment are in harmony.

The FLOW Quadrants

	Fulfilling Life (Low)	Fulfilling Life (High)
Optimizing Wealth (High)	ROI (Return on Investment)	ROI & ROL
Optimizing Wealth (Low)		ROL (Return on Life)

Aligning Finances with Life Goals

A story stands out because it illustrates the true essence of the FLOW framework. About two decades ago, this couple had big dreams but also many uncertainties about the future. The husband owned a successful business; they were pulled in different directions.

They had multiple priorities. On one hand, they wanted to secure their financial future, including long-term care, asset protection, and a business exit. On the other hand, they were deeply family-oriented, wishing to provide for their children and create a legacy for future generations. They were also passionate about giving back and wanted to ensure their wealth could make a difference in the world.

At first, their focus was mainly on the numbers. But numbers alone don't tell the whole story. The first challenge was clarifying a vision for life after the business. Like many business owners, they had spent decades pouring energy into their company and hadn't paused to ask, "What does life look like once the business is gone?"

This is a common issue. Research shows that 75% of business owners regret selling their business within one year of the exit. (Source: Exit Planning Institute, 2023 National State of Owner Readiness Report.)

Using a Fulfilling Life process, they dug deep, reflecting on questions such as:

- If you were financially secure, how would you live your life?
- Imagine you had 5–10 years left to live. What would you change about your life?
- Would you have regrets if your life ended tomorrow?
- What are the essential elements for you to live a fulfilling life?
- What obstacles can stand in the way? How would you overcome them?

The answers didn't come easily at first. Each spouse first envisioned an ideal future independently, then they brought those visions together and aligned them. For them, this life included traveling with family, hosting annual reunions, dedicating time to charitable causes, and even starting a small side business to stay engaged and fulfilled. Once their vision was clarified, they identified core values and used them to guide future decisions, creating the clarity needed to move forward to the Optimizing Wealth phase.

One of the first challenges was addressing long-term care. Like many people, they underestimated the risks. It's a sensitive topic—few want to think about aging or potential health issues. After honest conversations and quantifying the risks, they explored ways to manage or transfer them.

Their wealth included substantial real-estate holdings, so attention turned to protecting these assets—safeguarding what had been built over a lifetime while ensuring it could support future goals.

As life circumstances evolved, so did their legacy goals. They became even more charitably inclined and wanted to donate to causes close to their hearts, while balancing lifestyle needs. Their estate attorney updated their plan so assets would pass smoothly to their children and reflect their charitable wishes.

Taxes were another major consideration. They coordinated with tax advisors to allocate wealth efficiently across taxable, tax-deferred, and tax-free accounts. Managing withdrawals and optimizing tax strategy helped maximize flexibility while minimizing the tax burden.

Transitioning from the accumulation phase to the distribution phase was a significant adjustment. During the accumulation phase, the primary goal was growth. In the distribution phase, the focus shifted to balancing liquidity, safety, income, and continued growth. A distribution strategy tailored to their needs was developed—designed to help sustain their wealth and support their vision for the future. This included setting aside funds for specific goals, like hosting annual family reunions and funding vacations.

The transition wasn't without challenges. Like many business owners, stepping away from the company raised fears about identity and purpose. Those concerns were addressed through Fulfilling Life exercises that helped reconnect purpose beyond the business.

Today, this couple has fully embraced the FLOW framework. Their financial strategies align with their life goals, and planning has extended to include their children—supporting a multigenerational vision for legacy.

They now host family reunions every year, travel regularly, and contribute generously to causes they care about. The shift has been from a life centered on work to one centered on what truly matters: family, values, and fulfillment.

This story offers lessons for anyone seeking to align finances with personal goals and dreams.

Footnote: This client story is based upon the experience of a client of Ameriprise Financial Services, LLC, and is unpaid. The experience described may not be representative of the experience of other clients and is not a guarantee of future performance or success. As a client of Ameriprise Financial, you may work with different financial advisors at any time.

Lesson 1: Planning Is Never Too Early or Too Late

It's never too early or too late to start planning. Of course, starting earlier is better—it gives you more time and flexibility—but even if you feel like you've waited too long, there's still time to make meaningful changes. As the proverb goes, "When the student is ready, the teacher will appear." This client's readiness to explore their future and their willingness to embrace a new approach to financial planning made all the difference. The same is true for you—once you open yourself up to the possibilities, the right path will present itself.

Lesson 2: Always Start with the "Why"

The FLOW framework emphasizes starting with your why. This client's success hinged on defining their life goals before diving into the financial details. Once they clarified their vision for the future—traveling with family, hosting reunions, giving to charity—the "what" and "how" became much easier to address.

Lesson 3: Align Financial Decisions with Core Values

This client found peace and confidence in their financial choices because every decision reflected who they were and what mattered most to them. When you make financial decisions that resonate with your values, you're less likely to second-guess yourself. You're also more likely to stay committed to those decisions because they authentically express who you are.

Lesson 4: Financial Planning Must Be Comprehensive

Financial planning isn't just about investments or savings. Many components include risk management, estate planning, tax strategies, and personal goals. This client's journey shows how vital it is to address all these aspects in a cohesive way.

Lesson 5: Plan for the Long Term—But Stay Flexible

I often tell clients, "Plan your life as if you'll live forever, but live your life as if you'll die tomorrow." This client embraced that mindset by setting long-term goals while remaining adaptable to life's uncertainties. Life is unpredictable, and your plan needs to reflect that. The ability to adjust and adapt to changes in health, family dynamics, or financial markets is crucial to sustaining your wealth and fulfillment.

Lesson 6: Financial Planning Is a Team Sport

This client's success wasn't achieved in isolation. Financial planning is a team sport that requires collaboration between you, your family, and your advisors. We worked closely with their legal and tax advisors to ensure their plan was aligned and optimized. Just as importantly, we involved their family in the process. Financial planning should create a fulfilling life for everyone involved.

Life Comes First, Money Comes Next

At its core, the FLOW framework reminds us of one simple yet profound truth: Life comes first, and money comes next. Whether you're managing your personal finances or transitioning from a business you've built, the guiding principle remains the same—your life should lead, and your money should follow.

At the same time, planning for the long term doesn't mean ignoring life's unpredictability. Plan for the worst, but live for the best. Build your defense first, so you can play offense with confidence. Knowing you're prepared for risks allows you to live fully without fear of what tomorrow might bring.

Remember that none of us can do this alone. If you're retiring for the first time or navigating complex financial decisions, there's no shame in asking for professional help. It's a sign of strength. Think of financial planning as a team sport. You are the architect and CEO of your life, but you don't have to do everything yourself. Surround yourself with a trusted team—your financial, legal, and tax advisors. Delegate the technical work so you can focus on living your vision.

Life is short. Be bold, plan with purpose, and live with intention. When your finances flow effortlessly toward the life you envision, you achieve not just a return on investment but a true return on life.

KEY TAKEAWAYS

- Financial life planning starts with understanding your "why." Aligning your money with your life goals and values ensures that your financial decisions are meaningful and purposeful.
- The FLOW mindset emphasizes Fulfilling Life and Optimizing Wealth, blending holistic vision with strategic financial action to create alignment between life and finances.
- Money is a tool, not a goal—its purpose is to empower you to live a fulfilling life, support your values, and create meaningful connections, not just to accumulate wealth for its own sake.
- Comprehensive financial planning includes managing risks, planning for legacy and taxes, and ensuring your investments support your broader life vision, all while staying adaptable to life's uncertainties.
- Financial planning is a collaborative process involving trusted advisors and your family to create a holistic strategy that empowers you to live boldly and intentionally, achieving a return on investment *and* a return on life.

Chapter TWO

Pacing Your Financial Journey to Natural Rhythms

"Nature does not hurry, yet everything is accomplished."

– Lao Tzu

Thinking about financial life planning or wealth planning can feel overwhelming. You might not know where to start because it touches so many different areas of life. That's completely understandable. But here's what I've learned: your financial plan should adapt to you. It should follow you through life, evolving as your needs, goals, and priorities change.

Where are you in life right now? Are you in your peak earning years, looking to maximize retirement contributions and catch-up opportunities? Are you preparing for retirement and figuring out how to transition into a new phase of life? Or are you managing your retirement distributions and focusing on preserving your legacy?

Most people I work with are in the pre-retirement phase, transitioning into retirement, or early or late retirement. Each stage requires a different financial approach, aligning your financial plan with your life's natural rhythm.

Pre-Retirement

Before you retire, ask yourself: What does retirement actually look like for you? Too often, I've seen business owners sell their companies and professionals retire from their careers, thinking they're financially set, only to regret it within a year because they had no "life after" plan. Their work defined them, and without it, they felt lost. At this stage, it's critical to develop passions and connections outside of work so that you don't feel adrift when you retire.

Financially, this period often involves reviewing debt, cash flow, and whether projected income aligns with spending goals. For business owners, exit planning is typically part of the process. Identifying any projected gap before a sale provides time to evaluate adjustments; outcomes are not assured, but this planning can inform decisions and help address the risk of retirement shortfalls.

Another key aspect of pre-retirement planning is shifting your mindset from accumulation to distribution. Many people focus solely on saving, but retirement requires a strategy for drawing from those savings in a sustainable way. A well-thought-out distribution plan that helps make a smooth financial transition when the time comes.

Early Retirement

The first few years of retirement bring some of the biggest financial and emotional adjustments. Many people experience five phases of retirement: pre-retirement, the honeymoon phase, disenchantment, reorientation, and stability. While the honeymoon phase is exciting, with newfound freedom and the ability to finally do what you want, it often comes with increased spending. Travel, hobbies, and entertainment become priorities, but without a financial plan in place, that excitement can lead to overspending.

Soon after, the disenchantment phase sets in. Many retirees find themselves feeling bored, unfulfilled, or even depressed. I recommend taking this time to build new routines and explore new hobbies. Volunteering, taking on new experiences, or even working part-time will greatly impact your overall happiness.

You want to enjoy this phase of life without outliving your money, so focus on balancing your spending and managing your taxes. This is also the time to get serious about healthcare and long-term care planning, as medical expenses can become a significant factor in later years.

Late Retirement

By the time you reach late retirement, you've likely established a routine and settled into your new lifestyle. Many people move during this phase to be closer to family, downsize, or transition into assisted living. These changes often bring adjustments such as managing new housing costs, adapting to healthcare needs, or reevaluating long-term care options.

This is also when legacy planning comes into play. At this stage, wealth transfer becomes more tangible, and many people start thinking about gifting, charitable donations, or estate planning. However, one of the biggest mistakes I see is people giving away too much too soon without ensuring their own long-term care costs are fully covered. Generosity is wonderful, but financial security should always come first.

Life Events That Require Financial Adjustments

Regardless of where you are in life, unexpected events happen. Your financial plan needs to be flexible enough to adapt. Marriage, divorce, career changes, child or grandchild births, and family transitions can impact financial stability. Any major change requires a fresh look at your finances to ensure your wealth continues to support your evolving life.

The Two Meanings of Natural Rhythms

When I talk about natural rhythms in financial planning, I mean it in two ways.

First, there's **the rhythm of your life stages.** Your financial priorities in your 40s won't be the same as they are in your 70s. As you move from accumulating wealth to distributing it, your investments, insurance, tax planning strategies, and estate plans all need to shift accordingly. Yet, I see so many people who haven't adjusted their financial plans to reflect their new reality. If your wealth isn't aligned with your life stage, it isn't truly serving you.

The second meaning of natural rhythm is **the cadence of financial planning throughout the year**. I've found that when people are given a massive to-do list covering 20 different areas, they get overwhelmed and procrastinate. Instead, I've developed a seasonal approach to financial planning, breaking it into smaller, more manageable steps that fit naturally into the flow of life.

Think about it. Every year, we already follow financial rhythms without realizing it. We all file tax returns in the first part of the year. At year-end, we naturally look at things like tax-loss harvesting or charitable donations. By structuring financial planning around these existing rhythms, it becomes easier, more intuitive, and—most importantly—more likely to get done.

I've spent over two decades working with clients, and I can tell you that **financial planning works best when it follows a natural flow**. That's why I break the year into different financial "seasons" to help people implement their plans without stress.

- **Goal Tracking Season** – Reviewing progress, verifying assumptions, and setting objectives for the year ahead.
- **Investment & Insurance Season** – Evaluating wealth management, asset allocation, and protection strategies. While investments are reviewed in every season, this season provides an in-depth analysis of investment strategies.
- **Year-End Strategy Season** – Tax planning, gifting, charitable donations, retirement contribution/distribution, estate updates, etc.

Now, you can celebrate milestones instead of stressing over an endless to-do list. The key here is **habit stacking**—a concept even popularized in books like *Atomic Habits*. When you break large objectives into smaller actions, you create momentum. As you achieve one milestone, you gain confidence to tackle the next. This approach also fosters a growth mindset—as you see progress, you may find yourself thinking, *If I can accomplish this, maybe I can do even more.* And because the process is structured in steps, you can course-correct along the way without feeling like you've fallen behind.

The Head and Heart Returns

I always encourage clients to recognize two kinds of financial returns: the **head** and **heart returns**.

The **head return** is straightforward—it's the measurable side of financial planning. You track savings, investments, withdrawal rates, and tax efficiencies here. We conduct an annual review to assess whether your current trajectory is sustainable. If you're withdrawing funds, we look at last year's percentage and project forward—will this withdrawal rate work for the next ten, twenty, or thirty years? Will your investments continue to generate enough income? Are you minimizing taxes? These are all critical questions that help us gauge your return on wealth.

But the **heart return** is just as important—if not more so. Numbers alone don't tell the whole story of financial success. The real question is: How do you feel about your financial situation? Do you feel confident? Are you at peace knowing your wealth is supporting your fulfilling life? Are you able to have stress-free conversations with your spouse about money? Have you successfully passed down financial habits to the next generation?

The heart return is about how well your financial plan aligns with your life. Can you travel without worrying about outliving your money? Do you have the resources and time to care for elderly parents? Can you support charitable causes that matter to you? When both the head and the heart are in harmony, that's when you can genuinely celebrate progress.

Heart return is equivalent to Return On Life (ROL), a measure of Fulfilling Life. Head return is equivalent to Return On Investment (ROI), a measure of Optimizing Wealth. When you have both ROL and ROI, you are in FLOW.

How Small Wins Keep You on Track

Because financial planning is long-term—sometimes stretching beyond your lifetime—it can feel intangible. This makes it easy to feel disconnected from the process, leading to hesitation, procrastination, or even avoidance. But recognizing small victories along the way can keep you motivated.

Take life insurance and long-term care insurance, for example. Most people recognize that transferring financial risk through insurance is a smart decision. Yet, when faced with premium payments, they hesitate. They see it as an expense rather than an investment in financial security. But when we take a step back and evaluate cash flow, we can often restructure spending or investments to make the cost manageable. A year later, many clients tell me, *"I barely noticed the payments, but now I have peace of mind."* That's a financial victory worth celebrating.

Another example is automating financial habits. Many books, including *Atomic Habits* and *Automatic Retirement*, emphasize the power of making financial discipline second nature. When saving, investing, and even insurance payments become automated, they stop feeling like sacrifices and start feeling like routine. Over time, this builds a strong financial foundation without added stress.

I also see this with clients transitioning into retirement. One of the biggest concerns I hear is, *"How do I balance enjoying my money now while still ensuring I have enough for the future?"* This is where we introduce a bucket strategy—dividing assets into short-term, intermediate, and long-term buckets. The short-term bucket covers current expenses, the intermediate bucket provides stability, and the long-term bucket focuses on growth. Once clients see that their short-term needs are secure and their future money is still compounding, they feel empowered. The discipline of planning their withdrawals becomes rewarding rather than restrictive.

The Power of Seeing Progress

A business owner had built a successful company but was uncertain about the financial future. The goal was to exit the business and retire in five years, but it wasn't clear whether that timeline was realistic. Like many business owners, there wasn't a clear number in mind—how much would be needed to retire comfortably, support a desired lifestyle, or sustain family needs. The central question was whether five years was realistic or if working longer would be necessary.

The first step was to identify and quantify personal and family life goals. Where would the family live? How often would they travel? Would ongoing support be provided for children's or grandchildren's education? Once lifestyle goals were clarified, the **freedom gaps** were calculated—the differences between current resources and what would be needed to make retirement viable. This wasn't a single number; multiple scenarios were outlined:

- The **bare-minimum** number covered essential needs with limited flexibility for travel, experiences, or giving.
- A **more fulfilling** retirement required additional resources, allowing life to be enjoyed on the family's terms.
- A **comprehensive** plan incorporated buffers for unexpected expenses—health care, market downturns, or business disruptions.
- A **legacy-focused** number reflected the desire to provide for heirs and charitable causes.

Next, risks that could disrupt the plan were identified. What if a disability or a health issue arose? What if the business had to be dissolved due to unforeseen challenges? What if disagreements emerged among partners or family members? These risks were addressed early; appropriate insurance options and contingency plans were evaluated to help protect what had been built.

With goals and risk considerations established, a cash-flow strategy was developed to increase retirement savings. Savings targets were broken into quarterly, monthly, and annual milestones to make progress steady and manageable. Funds were allocated strategically—across tax-deferred, taxable, and tax-free accounts—based on the long-term picture.

Over time, retirement savings increased, risk protections were put in place, and business value improved. Although retiring had been the original plan, the owner chose to remain involved because cash flow was strong, and family members became engaged in continuing the legacy. Importantly, the business moved toward being sale-ready, creating greater optionality and a sense of control over timing. Progress was tracked and reviewed annually, with adjustments made as needed, which increased confidence in the plan and the path forward. This illustrates the power of breaking big goals into manageable milestones: uncertainty gives way to a clearer decision framework and more options for retiring on one's terms, step by step.

Whether you're in pre-retirement, transitioning into a new phase of life, or already well into retirement, the key is staying proactive and adaptable. Your financial strategy should evolve with you so that your wealth continues to serve your life—not the other way around. By putting a written financial plan in place and reviewing it regularly with a trusted advisor, you can gain greater peace of mind, knowing your decisions align with your vision and each step moves you toward a fulfilling future.

Footnote: This client story is based upon the experience of a client of Ameriprise Financial Services, LLC, and is unpaid. The experience described may not be representative of the experience of other clients and is not a guarantee of future performance or success. As a client of Ameriprise Financial, you may work with different financial advisors at any time.

KEY TAKEAWAYS

- Your financial plan should evolve with your life's natural rhythms, adapting to your changing needs, priorities, and goals at each stage.
- Pre-retirement is the time to prepare mentally and financially. You must have a clear vision for life after work, a sustainable withdrawal strategy, and a plan to transition from accumulation to distribution.
- Early retirement often brings excitement but also unexpected emotional and financial adjustments. Thoughtful planning around spending, healthcare, and meaningful engagement helps create a fulfilling and financially stable transition.
- Late retirement shifts focus to preserving wealth and simplifying finances. Maintaining sustainable income and funding healthcare are critical priorities. As you organize finances for current needs and future heirs, estate planning takes center stage.
- Breaking financial planning into seasonal rhythms—goal tracking, investment reviews, and estate planning—makes it more manageable, reduces stress, and builds momentum for long-term success.
- True financial success balances both head returns (measurable wealth growth) and heart returns (confidence, fulfillment, and financial peace of mind), ensuring your money serves your life at every stage.

Chapter THREE

Overcoming Biases and Blind Spots

"You can't read the label from inside the jar."
- Dan Sullivan

A common assumption is that financial planning is a straightforward, logical process—if you're advised to do *A*, you'll do *A*, and *A* will naturally lead to *B*. But that's not how it works. We're human. We're emotional. And whether we realize it or not, our decisions aren't always rational. They're shaped by our past experiences, personal beliefs, stress levels, and even what's happening on any given day. Biases and blind spots influence how we approach money; if we don't acknowledge them, they can prevent us from making the right financial moves.

I became a behavioral finance advisor because I saw firsthand how human behavior impacts financial outcomes. Research supports this. The most recent DALBAR research on investor behavior, published in April 2025, revealed that behavioral missteps caused average equity investors to underperform the S&P 500 by 8.48%

in 2024. This lag is a result of imprudent investor decisions and is a manifestation of the well-documented "investor behavior gap." Your mindset and decision-making have a far greater impact on your wealth than the specific investments you choose.

Early in my career, I assumed that once I helped map out a sound financial plan for clients, they would simply follow it. I'd analyze their current situation, understand their goals, identify the gaps, and recommend strategies to get them there. But time and again, I watched people make irrational decisions that completely undermined their long-term financial success. Instead of sticking to the plan, they'd get distracted by short-term gratification. They'd forget their goals. They'd rationalize impulsive spending or make emotional investment choices. As an advisor, it was frustrating to see such apparent mistakes—mistakes that were entirely avoidable.

Vanguard's Advisor's Alpha research found that **financial advisors can potentially add "up to, or even exceed, 3% in net returns."** It estimates that **behavioral coaching can contribute up to 1.5%-2%** of the total potential 3% net returns added by financial advisors annually. (Source: Vanguard Advisor's Alpha Research, 2022.)

The Most Common Biases That Impact Financial Decision-Making

If you remember from the previous chapter, we talked about *heart return* versus *head return*. That concept applies here, too. Emotional biases stem from feelings, intuition, and impulse, while cognitive biases are rooted in flawed reasoning and mental shortcuts. Both can interfere with financial decision-making, but emotional biases are often more difficult to correct because they are deeply ingrained in our identity and personal history.

I see these biases play out every single day—not just in clients but in myself, too. And they're not limited to finances. They show up in how we communicate with our spouses, how we parent, and even in small decisions like grocery shopping. We all have biases because we're human, and they shape how we interpret the world.

In fact, my son has even caught me in a bias before, saying, *"Mom, that was confirmation bias."* And he was right! These patterns are everywhere, and if we don't recognize them, they can lead us to make irrational financial choices. Here are the ones I see most often.

Confirmation Bias: Seeing What We Want to See

Confirmation bias is one of the biggest culprits. It happens when we form an opinion—consciously or subconsciously—and then seek out information that supports it while ignoring anything that contradicts it. Ever notice how, when you buy a red car, suddenly you start seeing red cars everywhere? Or when you're pregnant, you notice more pregnant women? That's your brain filtering information to confirm what it already believes.

In financial planning, this bias leads people to justify decisions they've already made, even if those decisions aren't in their best interest. They'll find articles, experts, or even friends who validate their thinking while dismissing any advice that challenges their perspective.

Recency Bias: The Trap of Short-Term Thinking

Recency bias is our tendency to give more weight to the most recent events rather than looking at the bigger picture. For example, if the stock market had a great year, people assumed it would keep going up. If it had a bad year, they panicked, convinced that the downturn would never end. They forgot history; the market has always had ups and downs. Instead, they latch onto whatever just happened and believe, *"This time is different."*

But the truth is, it's never really different. Every financial crisis, boom, and crash has happened before in some form. Those who remember history can avoid making reactionary decisions based on short-term fear or excitement.

Loss Aversion: The Fear of Losing More Than We Can Handle

Loss aversion is one of the most substantial biases I observe among investors. People are far more affected by losses than they are by gains of the same size. For example, if someone loses $100,000 in the stock market, their emotional pain is significantly greater than the excitement they'd feel if they gained that same $100,000. Even though the dollar amounts are the same, the impact isn't. This is why people panic-sell during downturns. They hit a mental threshold—maybe it's losing $100,000 or $500,000—and suddenly, fear takes over. They convince themselves they have to pull out, even when logic and history suggest staying the course.

Anchoring Bias: Fixating on a Number That No Longer Matters

Anchoring bias happens when people get stuck on a specific number—usually the highest peak their portfolio ever reached. I always hear this: *"At one point, my investments were worth X."* In their mind, that number becomes their reference point, their anchor. It doesn't matter that the market fluctuates daily or that their portfolio was only at that high for a brief moment—they fixate on that number and compare everything to it. It's like looking at the hottest temperature ever recorded in your city and expecting it always to be that hot. That peak was an outlier, not a baseline. But when people anchor to it, they set unrealistic expectations for their investments, leading to disappointment and poor financial decisions.

Status Quo Bias: The Cost of Doing Nothing

Then there's status quo bias, which is simply inertia—the tendency to avoid change because it feels uncomfortable. I see this, especially with prospective clients who have never worked with a financial planner before. They tell me, *"I'm doing fine. Why change anything?"* They resist taking action, not because their plan is working, but because they're used to their current situation. The problem is that the pain of not changing hasn't outweighed the pain of change—yet. But by the time it does, it's often too late to correct the course. They've lost valuable time and opportunities simply because they were afraid to make a move.

Overconfidence Bias: "I'm Smart Enough to Do It Myself."

I've worked with brilliant clients—physicists, doctors, engineers—who believe that because they excel in their field, they can easily manage their finances on their own. Their emotional confidence makes them feel they don't need financial advice, but their cognitive bias comes from misunderstanding risk or failing to interpret financial data correctly. They assume intelligence in one area transfers to another, which can lead to costly mistakes.

Cognitive Dissonance

Happens when people struggle with conflicting financial beliefs. A client might have been raised to believe one thing about money, but now they're hearing conflicting advice from financial media or professionals. This internal conflict creates anxiety, making it hard for them to commit to a financial plan. At the same time, the cognitive side of the bias comes into play when they are presented with two sets of numbers or data that seem to contradict each other. Without clarity, they hesitate to act.

How to Overcome Biases

Because cognitive biases are rooted in flawed thinking, they can often be corrected by presenting clear, accurate information. Once a client sees data that challenges their assumptions, they can adjust their decision-making process. Emotional biases, however, are much harder to "fix." Instead of forcing change, a better approach is acknowledging them and adapting financial strategies accordingly.

We help our clients overcome their biases by breaking financial decisions into smaller, manageable steps. When people take action in small increments, they feel less overwhelmed and start to build confidence. Each milestone helps reinforce better decision-making, helping to shift both cognitive and emotional patterns gradually.

A Scientist's Blind Spot: Overconfidence in a Fixed Formula

One of the most memorable examples of a financial blind spot involved a brilliant scientist—a PhD, extremely intelligent, highly analytical, and well-read. He understood risk at a deep level and had developed his own formula for managing investments. In his mind, as long as he followed this formula, he believed it would produce a specific rate of return over the long term.

Because he was so confident in his calculations, he took a highly aggressive approach to investing. He believed risk was just a numbers game, something he could manage purely through logic. But over time, his blind spot became clear: he never adjusted his risk strategy as he aged. Early in life, higher risk may be more tolerable because there is time to recover from market fluctuations. Later, financial priorities often shift—from wealth accumulation to wealth preservation and income generation. Despite this, he refused to change his approach. His mindset remained stuck in the same ratios and formulas he had followed for decades, without considering how his stage in life affected his liquidity needs.

Overconfidence became both an emotional and cognitive bias. Emotionally, he believed his intelligence and past success would continue to work in his favor. Cognitively, he was anchored to a fixed formula, ignoring new data that suggested a different approach might serve him better.

Addressing this blind spot took nearly a decade of small, incremental changes. On the cognitive side, the data were presented in a way that resonated with him. Historical market trends illustrated that his asset allocation did not align with what he believed. The conversation was reframed in terms of legacy, posing the question: If the goal is to leave this amount to a daughter, is the current level of risk really the best way to support that? Viewed through that lens, he began to reconsider.

On the emotional side, risk tolerance versus risk capacity was reassessed. He identified as an aggressive investor, but risk tolerance reflects comfort with uncertainty, while risk capacity reflects the ability to absorb losses and still meet goals. When income is needed from investments, there may no longer be the capacity to take the same level of risk—even if someone still thinks of themselves as aggressive.

Change did not happen overnight, but gradually, he began making adjustments. At first, a portion of the portfolio shifted to a more balanced strategy while a smaller "pocket" of aggressive investments remained. Over time, more of the rigid formulas were set aside, and a more flexible, professionally guided investment philosophy was adopted.

Despite the initial resistance, the evolution was notable. He later said something that revealed growth: "I know sometimes I make dumb decisions. You have my permission to call me out."

That level of self-awareness requires emotional intelligence. It isn't easy to admit when we're wrong, especially when we pride ourselves on our knowledge. Yet the wisest people recognize their own blind spots and seek out professionals who can challenge their thinking when needed.

Footnote: This client story is based upon the experience of a client of Ameriprise Financial Services, LLC, and is unpaid. The experience described may not be representative of the experience of other clients and is not a guarantee of future performance or success. As a client of Ameriprise Financial, you may work with different financial advisors at any time.

Techniques for Identifying Your Own Financial Biases and Blind Spots

The first and most important step in overcoming financial biases is humility. Without it, there's no willingness to listen, learn, or adjust. An old Chinese saying is, "*The far side of wisdom is ignorance.*"

The more we know, the more we realize we *don't* know. Teenagers often think they know everything, but as we age, we start to understand just how much we still have to learn. That, to me, is wisdom.

Here are some practical techniques to help uncover and address financial blind spots.

Track Your Decisions and Their Outcomes

One of the simplest ways to identify financial biases is to track your decision-making patterns. Each time you make a financial choice, write it down. Then, track the outcome. Did things turn out the way you expected? If not, why?

I've said this to my children, "Wise people learn from other people's mistakes, regular people learn from their *own* mistakes, and dumb people don't learn at all." The goal is to move from learning the hard way to learning the *smart* way by spotting patterns in our decisions before they become costly.

Align Decisions with Core Values

Another powerful technique is to check if your financial choices align with your core values. In behavioral finance, we discuss the *current self* versus the *ideal self.* Your ideal self is the version of you that makes decisions in alignment with your deepest values—whether that's independence, integrity, meaningful work, or financial security.

When facing a major financial decision, take a step back and ask:

- *Does this decision reflect my core values?*
- *Am I acting in a way that brings me closer to my ideal self?*

By taking this approach, financial decisions become more intentional and less reactive.

Make Decisions in the Right Emotional State

Emotions play a huge role in financial choices, which is why timing matters. Imagine a grid with four quadrants:

- **High positive energy** – Excitement, exuberance
- **High negative energy** – Anxiety, anger
- **Low positive energy** – Calm, contentment
- **Low negative energy** – Depression, self-doubt

The best financial decisions happen when we are in a *low-positive-energy* state—calm, clear-headed, and logical. The worst financial decisions happen when we are in a *high emotional state,* whether positive (euphoric investing) or negative (panic-selling). A *low negative emotional state* can lead to inaction or inertia.

To help avoid emotionally driven mistakes, create a decision tree ahead of time. When markets crash, do you panic and sell everything? When stocks soar, do you chase trends? Instead of reacting in the moment, set up clear guidelines in advance. This is why investment policies exist—to take the emotion out of decision-making.

Focus on Long-Term Vision, Not Short-Term Reactions

People make better financial decisions when they zoom out and think in terms of *years* rather than *moments.* If you envision your life 10, 15, or 20 years down the road, what decisions will help you get there? Knee-jerk reactions are rarely good long-term strategies. Every year, we revisit our clients' visions during Goal Tracking season. Are they still on track? Have their priorities shifted? Aligning money with long-term vision prevents emotional, short-term mistakes. At the same time, having the appropriate amount of short-term safety and liquidity investment helps them stay on course.

Regularly Reassess Risk Tolerance

Risk tolerance changes throughout life. A person who was aggressive at 35 might feel completely different at 65 when retirement is near. I've had clients who always identified as "aggressive investors" until they reached a stage in life where they needed a stable income. Their risk tolerance (how much uncertainty they could emotionally handle) hadn't changed, but their risk capacity (how much risk they could afford) had shifted dramatically. That's why risk tolerance should be reassessed regularly.

Work with Someone Who Can Challenge Your Biases

One of the best ways to overcome financial blind spots is to have a trusted sounding board, such as a financial advisor, a spouse, or even an adult child who can provide an outside perspective. Some of my older clients bring their adult children into financial meetings to ensure that big decisions align with their long-term family goals. Having someone else in the room adds a layer of accountability and helps prevent emotionally driven mistakes.

Remember that it all starts with humility—the willingness to acknowledge that we all have blind spots. It continues with education—learning from our own experiences and the insights of others. And it thrives on long-term thinking—staying focused on the bigger picture rather than reacting to short-term emotions.

Overcoming the Fear of Loss: A Journey to Financial Security

It's common to see investors sit on far more cash than they need for liquidity or security. Some sell a house or a business and—paralyzed by fear—leave the proceeds idle. One investor inherited a sizable amount of cash and wasn't sure what to do. A status quo bias took hold: holding the money felt safest, especially while cash earned decent interest.

Planning discussions focused on cash flow first, not just investments. The analysis showed that money needed to be aligned with future needs, not left indefinitely in a single account. Finances were organized into three clear buckets:

- **Short-Term Bucket** – Strategic cash for roughly the next three years, covering emergencies, living expenses, and immediate liquidity needs. This provided greater peace of mind within a written plan.
- **Medium-Term Bucket** – Moderately conservative investments intended to seek returns above inflation while remaining reasonably accessible in the near future.
- **Long-Term Bucket** – Growth-oriented investments with a 7+ year horizon to support long-term objectives—even in retirement.

Seeing the logic of the structure, the investor became more comfortable allocating beyond cash. This wasn't about taking blind risk; it was an informed decision to align wealth with both security and growth needs.

To address another concern—the "what ifs" of life—planning also evaluated and implemented protections, including options such as long-term care coverage. By addressing these contingencies within the plan, decisions were no longer driven by fear.

The plan was then tied back to core values—stability, independence, health, and relationships. The desire to be generous with family and to enjoy life had been constrained by fear of investing. Once money was aligned with those values, options opened up.

Over time, investing resumed and spending became more intentional. In one year, there was enough surplus to fund a family reunion trip. It wasn't an every-year event, but within a structured plan it was possible without drifting from long-term objectives.

Mastering the Human Side of Money

At its core, financial planning is about people. Money is quantitative, but we are emotional beings. Our fears, experiences, and biases shape our decisions in ways we often don't realize. And that's okay—it's what makes us human. Some people struggle with money because they feel guilty about wealth. Others have anxiety about making the wrong decisions. But the truth is, we all have financial biases. Even financial advisors aren't immune to them!

A valuable lesson in behavioral finance is that **financial success is more about our actions than our actual investments**. People often blame market fluctuations or low returns for their struggles, but in reality, poor financial habits—like overspending or failing to plan—have a much bigger impact than an extra 1-2% in returns.

The good news is that there are tools and strategies to help. Behavioral finance is a growing discipline with research-backed techniques to identify and correct biases. Financial planning isn't one-size-fits-all—it should be customized for **your** risk tolerance, life goals, and values.

Beyond personal finance, developing emotional intelligence around money can strengthen relationships. Spouses, business partners, and families all have different perspectives on wealth. Understanding behavioral finance can facilitate healthy financial conversations and help avoid conflicts caused by different money mindsets.

Ultimately, wisdom comes from self-awareness. Being open to learning, adapting, and seeking guidance is what separates those who struggle financially from those who thrive.

KEY TAKEAWAYS

- Our financial decisions are often driven more by behavior than by money management, with biases like confirmation bias, recency bias, and loss aversion shaping how we perceive risk and opportunity.
- Emotional biases are deeply ingrained and harder to correct than cognitive biases, making it essential to acknowledge them rather than try to eliminate them.
- Breaking financial choices into smaller steps, aligning money with core values, and making decisions in a calm emotional state can help overcome biases and lead to better outcomes.
- Financial success is less about picking the perfect investments and more about consistent, disciplined decision-making that aligns with long-term goals and values.
- Grow your self-awareness and emotional intelligence, and enroll someone who can be a wise sounding board to point out your blind spots, such as a professional or a financially responsible family member.

PART TWO

OPTIMIZING WEALTH FOR FINANCIAL FREEDOM (THE "WHAT")

Chapter FOUR

Your Individualized Path

"What is right for one soul may
not be right for another."
- Eileen Caddy

With so much financial advice available online, it's easy to assume you can create a solid financial plan by watching a YouTube video, reading an article, or using a financial calculator. Many people take a boilerplate approach—relying on simple rules of thumb like, "I need $2 million to retire" or "I can safely withdraw 3% of my savings." Others base their decisions on what a friend did, assuming their situation is identical.

This kind of thinking can be dangerous. It ignores individual circumstances, behaviors, and financial realities. A one-size-fits-all plan is not a real plan—it's just a rough estimate that fails to account for the unique complexities of your life.

Why Individualization Matters

In 2013, the Consumer Federation of America (CFA) and the CFP Board fielded a national survey that grouped U.S. households by planning approach:

1. Non-planners: do not engage in financial planning.
2. Limited planners: engage in only a few planning activities.
3. Basic planners: do some planning but without a comprehensive written plan.
4. Comprehensive planners: work with a professional and follow a written, detailed financial plan.

Key savings finding (self-reported in the survey):

61% of comprehensive planners reported saving at least 10% of income, compared with 36% of basic planners, 13% of limited planners, and 6% of non-planners.

(Footnote: Consumer Federation of America & CFP Board (2013). Financial Planning Profiles of American Households (Household Financial Planning Survey)

What this suggests: in this survey, households using a written, individualized planning approach were more likely to report higher saving behavior than those with informal or minimal planning. By contrast, informal or non-individualized approaches did not show the same association with higher reported saving rates. That gap often stems from assumptions: generic inputs can oversimplify key details and lead to less useful outputs. For example:

- **Inflation:** Many plans assume a fixed 3% inflation rate. But in recent years, inflation has fluctuated dramatically. A small change in this assumption can drastically alter retirement projections.

- **Taxes:** Most plans assume static tax rates, ignoring future changes in tax laws and how withdrawals from retirement accounts will be taxed.
- **Risk tolerance:** Many plans categorize investors as "moderate" or "conservative" based on a simple questionnaire. But real-world investing is more nuanced—some people tolerate market swings if they see potential gains, while others panic over any loss.

Clients often come to us with foundational plans they created on their own, but when we build a comprehensive, individualized plan, the results are rarely the same. This is why I use the term "financial planning" rather than "financial plan." A plan is static—by the time it's delivered, it's already outdated. Your circumstances evolve, markets shift, and your beliefs about money may change. A truly effective plan is an ongoing process that requires regular updates and adjustments. A plan made five years ago may no longer be relevant today.

For example:

- A car breaks down, requiring an unplanned expense.
- A new tax law affects how retirement withdrawals are taxed.
- A family decides to move to another state—or even another country—to be closer to loved ones or take advantage of lower living costs.

In my previous career as a management consultant for PricewaterhouseCoopers, I saw how Fortune 100 companies would hire consultants expecting best practices to apply across industries.

However, while companies may have similarities, their internal structures, challenges, and goals are never identical. Financial planning is even more complex because we deal with human behavior, family history, and emotional influences—elements that cannot be standardized.

People who don't individualize their plans usually fall into one of two extremes:

- **Oversimplification.** They assume all they need is a few numbers—income, retirement age, and savings rate—without considering deeper factors like spending habits, risk tolerance, or family needs.
- **Information Overload.** Others get overwhelmed by the sheer volume of financial advice and don't know what applies to them. They try to absorb everything but end up paralyzed, unsure of what steps to take.

The key is balance. Your plan should be detailed enough to reflect your unique situation but not so complex that it becomes overwhelming.

The Top Considerations in a Personalized Financial Plan

It all starts with understanding what a fulfilling life looks like for you. *Are you living a fulfilling life, or are you still striving for one?* Your circumstances, aspirations, and even past experiences shape your financial journey, and a plan should reflect those realities.

Culture

Certain families prioritize funding education for children and grandchildren, while others focus on travel or lifestyle experiences. Individuals who grew up in a third-world country carry deeply ingrained financial habits—either an aversion to spending due to past scarcity or a strong emphasis on supporting an extended family. In many Asian households, caring for aging parents is non-negotiable, even if it means sacrificing personal monetary goals. I understand this firsthand—my mother lives with me, and providing for her long-term care is part of my financial reality.

Family Dynamics

Family dynamics further complicate financial planning. Parents often assume a particular child will be responsible for providing support, but in reality, family roles are not always as clear-cut. We frequently help facilitate family wealth meetings to navigate these conversations, helping families address financial expectations for caregiving, inheritance, and long-term support.

Health Conditions

Some families have a history of longevity and expect to live well into their 90s, while others have a genetic predisposition to chronic illness. These realities shape retirement planning, long-term care strategies, and insurance decisions. Many people think they can secure long-term care insurance later in life, only to find that a new health diagnosis disqualifies them from coverage. Proactive planning ensures that these risks are addressed before they become problems.

Core Values and Priorities

This is especially important for couples, as differing priorities can create conflict. While one spouse may prioritize spending every last dollar in retirement, the other may want to ensure there's a financial legacy left behind. Even when priorities are aligned, the way each person defines them may differ. For example, both spouses may agree that estate planning is important, but one may see it as structuring finances to maximize personal independence, while the other views it as ensuring wealth is preserved for future generations. A financial planner must navigate these discussions, helping clients align their priorities and make decisions that reflect their shared and individual perspectives.

Behavioral and Emotional Influences

Cognitive biases like loss aversion can impact risk-taking and investment choices. A well-designed financial plan helps acknowledge these biases, ensuring that the strategies align with financial realities and the client's comfort level. Risk tolerance and risk capacity must be considered—while some individuals may emotionally resist risk, their financial situation may require a higher level of investment risk to meet long-term goals. Conversely, some people may feel comfortable taking significant risks, even when their financial circumstances don't support that level of exposure. Understanding these nuances helps create a plan that clients are more likely to follow.

Career and Income Variability

Business owners and self-employed individuals experience fluctuating earnings, making financial planning more complex than for salaried employees. Even those with steady incomes face risks losing a job can mean going from full income to zero overnight.

We plan for these uncertainties by incorporating safety nets and adaptable strategies.

Geographic Location

Many retirees consider moving to lower-cost areas or countries with more affordable healthcare and face challenges when local medical facilities fail to meet their needs. Others relocate to be closer to family, which can drastically shift housing expenses and tax considerations. Financial plans need to account for these possibilities so that major life transitions don't create financial strain.

Money Personality

Personality impacts financial behavior. Research by Russ Alan Prince identified nine high-net-worth personality types, each with different financial priorities. Some people are family stewards, prioritizing stability and legacy for future generations. Others value independence and autonomy, focusing on financial freedom rather than wealth accumulation. Some individuals are wealth accumulators, driven by the desire to grow their assets without necessarily having a plan for how to use them. Identifying these personalities helps tailor a plan that aligns with practical needs and psychological tendencies.

A successful financial plan aligns with both your head and your heart. When financial planning is approached this way, it becomes more than just numbers on a page—it becomes a roadmap for living the life you truly want.

Optimizing wealth is a technical aspect of planning, but it should never come at the expense of a fulfilling life. While investment returns and tax strategies are crucial, they should be balanced with a person's lifestyle needs and preferences. An individualized plan factors in investment preferences, such as socially responsible investing or avoiding certain financial products due to past negative experiences.

Your Financial Plan is a Living Path

Financial planning is a dynamic, evolving process that must adapt as life changes. The story of a successful engineer illustrates this. At first, he was single, highly independent, and focused on long-term investing. His primary goal was financial independence, and he was comfortable taking an aggressive investment approach. Then life changed: he got married, and his spouse decided not to work.

Suddenly, his financial responsibilities grew, and risk tolerance was reassessed. Life insurance was added to protect the new family, and education savings were introduced for future children.

An unexpected challenge followed—he was laid off. Without the safety net of a second income, the plan needed to pivot. An investment portfolio once designed for aggressive growth now required more liquidity. Assets were restructured, cash reserves set aside, and health-insurance coverage secured. A 401(k) was rolled into an IRA, and the lower-income period created an opportunity to consider Roth IRA conversions.

Over time, his career continued to shift. After another layoff, he began rethinking his entire path. With children in school and retirement savings on track, starting a business became a serious consideration—another major shift from salary to variable income. The plan incorporated additional protections so retirement goals wouldn't be jeopardized if the business didn't take off. Spending was adjusted, a cushion was built, and the move to self-employment was made with a clear fallback plan.

Then another life change—his mother became ill. Along with

siblings, he navigated the financial and emotional realities of long-term care. Supporting an aging parent required another adjustment as medical expenses and caregiving responsibilities entered the picture.

One thing remained constant: the plan was never static. It was reviewed and updated at each stage to help maintain financial stability through career shifts, family growth, and unforeseen events. Because investments were aligned with personal risk tolerance and risk capacity, discipline was maintained during market volatility. Ultimately, he felt prepared to retire on a timeline that fit his goals.

The lesson: everyone needs a plan—and, more importantly, that plan must be flexible. Life doesn't follow a straight line, and a financial strategy shouldn't either. If there is no written plan, consider creating one. If a plan hasn't been updated in years, consider a fresh look. The most effective plans anticipate change and stay aligned with what matters most.

Footnote: This client story is based upon the experience of a client of Ameriprise Financial Services, LLC, and is unpaid. The experience described may not be representative of the experience of other clients and is not a guarantee of future performance or success. As a client of Ameriprise Financial, you may work with different financial advisors at any time.

KEY TAKEAWAYS

- A one-size-fits-all approach to financial planning is ineffective—your plan must reflect your unique circumstances, values, and goals.
- A financial plan isn't a static document; it's an ongoing process that should evolve as your life changes, from career shifts to family needs.

- Avoid the extremes of oversimplification or information overload. Your plan should be detailed enough to be effective but not so complex that it becomes overwhelming.
- Your personal history, beliefs, and behaviors around money influence financial decisions and must be considered in your planning.
- The best financial plans are adaptable, ensuring security through life's uncertainties while staying aligned with your priorities.

Chapter FIVE

De-Risking to Protect Your Wealth

"An ounce of prevention is worth a pound of cure."
– Benjamin Franklin

Think of de-risking like a fence that gives you freedom. Imagine a group of kindergarteners laughing and running outside at a playground. But this playground is right next to a busy road. The moment they step outside the boundary, they're at risk. The solution is to build a fence. Once that fence is up, the kids can play freely without worry. Instead of limiting their freedom, it actually enhances it. That's exactly how financial protection works. People think creating a safety net will restrict them, but in reality, it gives them the freedom to enjoy life with peace of mind.

The Illusion of "I'm Fine"

Many people come to me saying, "I'm fine," because they assume everything will go as planned. But life doesn't work that way. Just yesterday, I had a conversation with someone who believed they were set for retirement until we factored in unexpected events.

What happens when:

- Your car breaks down?
- A health crisis drains your savings?
- A family emergency forces you to dip into your retirement funds?
- A policy change or economic downturn shifts the financial landscape?

If you only plan for the best, you're leaving yourself vulnerable. True financial security means anticipating these curveballs and having a plan in place before they happen. A financial plan isn't truly comprehensive unless it prepares for worst-case scenarios. By making smart choices and de-risking now, you won't have to live in fear of the "what-ifs."

The Risks You Need to Address

De-risking involves identifying what could go wrong, quantifying the potential impact, and implementing strategies to help mitigate the damage. When assessing risk, I divide it into two main categories: **personal risks** and **business risks**.

Personal Financial Risks

Let's explore the personal financial risks below using the R.I.S.K. acronym.

R: Relational and Health Risks

One of the most significant risks people face is **family risk**, which includes dying too soon or experiencing a serious illness. If you pass away unexpectedly, your loved ones could be left financially unprepared. On the other hand, living a long life but facing a chronic illness can lead to staggering medical expenses and depleting savings faster than expected.

I: Income and Longevity Risks

Income risk refers to the potential loss of your ability to earn a living due to disability, whether physical or mental. During your working years, particularly in your prime earning period, you are the "goose that lays the golden eggs." However, many people focus on protecting the "eggs"—their assets, like a house or car—while neglecting to protect the "goose"—themselves.

Longevity risk is essentially the opposite of dying too soon—you live longer than expected and run out of money. Many people assume they'll live to 85, but reaching 100 is becoming more common with medical advancements. Running out of savings late in life is one of the greatest fears for retirees, and it must be planned for.

S: Structural and Organizational Risks

A less obvious but equally damaging risk is **disorganization**. Many people have fragmented financial plans—investments in one place, insurance policies in another, and estate plans that don't align with anything. They make decisions in isolation, failing to see how all the pieces connect, putting them at risk of missing out on critical protections or paying more taxes than necessary.

Speaking of investments, another risk is **misalignment with your life goals.** If you need income in the short term, your investments should be structured conservatively. A more aggressive strategy might make sense if you have long-term growth goals. But too often, people make investment choices without fully understanding how they fit into the bigger picture.

K: Knowledge and Life Preservation Risks

Taxes are inevitable, but they shouldn't be a surprise. Yet many people fail to plan for tax law changes, missing possible opportunities to reduce their overall tax burden.

Then there's **legal risk**, particularly when it comes to estate planning. Without a proper plan, families often deal with confusion, disputes, and unnecessary tax burdens after a loved one's passing. I've seen families fall apart simply because there was no clear plan for distributing assets.

Finally, there's **market risk and liquidity risk**. The market will always go up and down. If your portfolio isn't structured to withstand volatility, you could suffer major losses at the worst possible time. And without a substantial cash reserve, even small unexpected expenses—like a home repair or medical bill—can throw your financial plan off track.

Business Risks: The Five Ds

Business risks can be divided into the "Five Ds," as defined by the Exit Planning Institute. These risks add another layer of complexity for business owners.

#1 & #2 DEATH & DISABILITY

One of the biggest threats is the sudden loss of a key player. If an owner or key employee dies or becomes disabled, the entire operation can be thrown into turmoil with no clear path for ownership transition or business continuity.

#3 DIVORCE

Divorce is a risk that many business owners overlook. A marital split can create financial instability and ownership disputes. I've worked with business owners who never considered how divorce could impact their company until they were forced to split assets or renegotiate partnerships. One business coach I know even starts client meetings with the question: *"How stable is your marriage?"* Because if a divorce happens, it could change everything.

#4 DISAGREEMENTS

Even among business partners, disagreements can cause serious disruptions. When multiple people own a business, they may have conflicting visions for its future, and without a clear agreement in place, these disagreements can lead to lawsuits or the dissolution of the company.

#5 DISTRESS

Distress can take many forms, including too much debt, economic downturns, political changes, or shifts in industry regulations.

For business owners, it's imperative to try to de-risk both personally and professionally. Addressing personal risks is the foundation, but ignoring business risks could mean losing everything you've built.

The De-Risking Process

The first step is to **identify** the risks that apply to you. As we've discussed, many people operate under the belief that *"It won't happen to me,"* but unexpected events happen all the time. The more you recognize potential threats, the better prepared you'll be.

Once you've identified risks, the next step is to **quantify** them. This is where science and statistics come in. For example, if you're evaluating long-term care risk, you can look at national and local averages—how long care typically lasts and how much it costs per day. When considering life insurance, calculate how much money your family would need to cover expenses, pay off debts, and maintain their living standards in the event of your unexpected or premature death. Business owners can look at the potential impact of losing a key employee or facing an economic downturn.

After quantifying the risks, the next step is to **evaluate** their *likelihood* and *severity*. Some risks are highly likely but not severe—like minor market fluctuations. Others, like premature death, may be less likely but come with severe consequences. The key is to determine which risks require immediate action and which can be handled through diversification, cash reserves, or insurance.

The likelihood and severity of a risk will guide your decision on how much to **transfer** and how much to **assume**. For highly severe risks, such as long-term care, premature death, or disability, it is often prudent to transfer at least a portion of the risk through insurance. Attempting to assume these risks entirely may be impractical and could potentially derail your financial plan completely.

With that understanding, it's time to implement solutions. Insurance is one tool, but it's not the only one. Life insurance, disability insurance, and long-term care policies can help transfer certain risks, but other strategies—like annuities, legal structures, and emergency cash reserves—are just as important. Estate plans, buy-sell agreements, and tax-efficient investment tactics also reduce overall financial exposure.

Keep in mind that de-risking isn't a one-time event. Your financial plan must evolve and adjust as tax laws change, markets shift, and personal circumstances evolve. What made sense for you ten years ago may not be the right strategy today.

Misconceptions About De-Risking

Many people avoid thinking about risk because it makes them uncomfortable, but ignoring it doesn't make it disappear. Let's break down some of the biggest misconceptions people have about de-risking.

"It's an Emotional Decision"

Many people avoid thinking about risk altogether. They tell themselves, *"That won't happen to me,"* or *"I'm not going to die or become disabled."* But risk management isn't based on feelings—it's based on probabilities. You don't have to *feel* at risk to *be* at risk. No one knows what will happen, but pretending risks don't exist is not a strategy.

"I Don't Want to Worry"

People often avoid planning for risk because they don't want to stress about worst-case scenarios. But the truth is, risk doesn't wait for the "right time." The earlier you plan, the more options you have. Unfortunately, many people wait until they feel they *need* coverage; by then, it's usually too late. No insurance company will cover you *after* you develop a major health condition. The time to prepare is before the risk becomes a reality.

"It's Too Expensive"

I hear this all the time: *"I can't afford long-term care insurance."* My response? *If you can't afford the premium, how will you afford the full cost?* If the premium is just a small fraction of the total expense, how will you pay 100% out of pocket? Planning for risk is cheaper than dealing with the consequences of being unprepared. Insurance and other risk-management tools provide leverage—small costs now can prevent massive financial loss later.

"I Don't Like Insurance or Annuities"

I've heard people reject financial protection strategies outright, saying, *"I don't like insurance,"* or *"Annuities aren't for me."* The problem isn't the products themselves—it's how they're used. There are no *bad* financial tools, just bad applications. If you don't take the time to identify and quantify your risks first, you might end up with coverage that doesn't fit your needs. Many people make the mistake of buying a product because a salesperson recommended it, not because it was part of a well-structured plan. Then, when it doesn't work as expected, they blame the product instead of the poor planning that led to the purchase.

"I Bought Life Insurance 20 Years Ago, So I'm Covered"

Many assume that once they purchase a policy, they never have to think about it again. But financial risk changes over time. Twenty years ago, your income, assets, and responsibilities were different. Maybe you didn't have to support aging parents back then, or your business wasn't as valuable as it is today.

That's why re-evaluating your protection strategy should be part of your regular planning. Every year, you should reassess your risks, update your coverage, and rebalance your investments to keep them aligned with your goals.

A Three-Generation Approach to De-Risking Wealth

A family spanning three generations illustrates how different risks can be addressed across time. Each generation faced distinct financial exposures. Through a combination of business-succession planning, insurance strategies, and estate restructuring, a coordinated plan was developed to help position wealth to support future generations.

In their 70s, the grandparents faced two key risks—potential long-term care expenses and estate-tax exposure tied to their business. Years earlier, the business had been placed into an irrevocable trust, which seemed prudent at the time. However, tax law changes meant that if the business remained in that trust at death, the next generation could inherit it without a step-up in cost basis, creating a substantial tax burden.

To address this, an experienced estate attorney petitioned the court to unwind the irrevocable trust. Ownership was then restructured in a manner intended to help minimize tax exposure.

The grandparents also purchased life insurance with a long-term care rider. The policy could help cover care costs if needed; if care were not required, the death benefit could pass to children and help offset estate-related obligations.

Given their age, investments were adjusted to reduce risk, making the portfolio more conservative. A portion of assets was allocated to an annuity to create an additional income stream in retirement.

The second generation—a couple in their 40s—had different priorities. With teenage children, one with special needs, their plan needed to address income protection and survivor income.

The primary earner obtained disability income protection to help safeguard household cash flow if work became impossible due to illness or injury. After evaluating term and permanent life insurance, a blend including a cash-value component was selected to support multiple goals:

- Provide financial protection for the family in the event of a parent's death.
- Offer potential cash-value accumulation that could be accessed in later years.
- Add another source of tax diversification.

A special needs trust was also established. Life-insurance proceeds were structured to fund the trust, supporting long-term financial security for the child with special needs.

The youngest generation—a teenage grandson with special

needs—faced a different risk: future insurability. Because qualifying for coverage might become difficult over time, coverage was arranged while he was still young. The policy offered a measure of financial flexibility for future needs—whether education, a first home, or long-term planning—and helped mitigate the risk of being locked out of coverage later due to medical history.

This family's story highlights the value of strategic de-risking. Each generation faced unique challenges, yet by coordinating succession planning, insurance, estate design, and investment adjustments, the overall strategy aimed to align risk management and legacy goals across time.

At its core, de-risking supports a fulfilling life and the optimization of wealth. Building a resilient financial defense can help people live more freely and keep wealth serving what matters most—for themselves and for those they love.

Footnote: This client story is based upon the experience of a client of Ameriprise Financial Services, LLC, and is unpaid. The experience described may not be representative of the experience of other clients and is not a guarantee of future performance or success. As a client of Ameriprise Financial, you may work with different financial advisors at any time.

KEY TAKEAWAYS

- De-risking is part of a written financial plan that's reviewed over time. Having that plan in place can provide greater peace of mind while giving you the flexibility to enjoy life without undue financial worry.
- Many believe they're financially secure until unexpected events like medical emergencies, economic downturns, or

family crises reveal vulnerabilities. True financial security requires planning for worst-case scenarios.

- De-risking involves identifying potential financial threats, quantifying their impact, determining how much risk to transfer versus how much to assume, and implementing strategies—such as insurance, estate planning, and diversified investments—to minimize exposure.
- Business owners face additional risks, such as death, divorce, and disputes, that can jeopardize their companies. Proactively addressing these risks ensures business continuity and long-term financial stability.
- A multi-generational approach to de-risking wealth helps protect families at every stage of life, securing financial well-being through thoughtful estate planning, insurance solutions, and investment strategies tailored to evolving needs.

Chapter SIX

Goal-Based Investing

"Money means nothing until it serves something meaningful."
- Violetta Terpeluk

The goal of investing isn't just to accumulate wealth—it's to align investments with life's purpose. Every financial decision should support the life you want to live. Many people think of investing only as a way to grow money or generate income, but that's an incomplete view.

Investments should be a vehicle—like a plane, a bike, or a car—getting you to your financial destination. Without a clear plan, investors may default to an emotional, short-term mindset—fluctuating between excessive risk and excessive caution. A tr example of a market-reactive investor shows why a structured, goals-based approach can help.

The Market-Reactive Investor

It's common for self-directed investors to make inconsistent investment choices—holding predominantly cash out of risk concerns or allocating heavily to aggressive equities during uptrends—with little middle ground or coherent strategy.

One investor exhibited this exact pattern: either primarily in cash or fully invested in aggressive equities, with decisions driven by headlines and short-term reactions. During the planning process, the three-bucket approach from Chapter Three was introduced:

- **Short-term bucket:** Cash reserves for immediate needs.
- **Intermediate-term bucket:** Investments designed for stability and income.
- **Long-term bucket:** Growth-focused investments for the future.

In this case, short-term cash was sufficient and the intermediate bucket provided income, allowing the long-term bucket to remain focused on growth. Because this structure was new, the investor closely monitored the portfolio and became anxious when the long-term bucket experienced normal market fluctuations. At check-ins, the plan reiterated: "Cash reserves are in place. The income bucket remains stable. The long-term bucket is designed to fluctuate because it is positioned for growth."

Over time, with consistent reviews against the written plan, the investor developed confidence in the process. Rather than making reactive decisions, investments were viewed as components of a coherent strategy—supporting long-term objectives.

Footnote: This client story is based upon the experience of a client of Ameriprise Financial Services, LLC, and is unpaid. The experience described may not be representative of the experience of other clients and is not a guarantee of future performance or success. As a client of Ameriprise Financial, you may work with different financial advisors at any time.

How Goal-Based Investing Differs from Traditional Investing

In earlier chapters, we discussed the difference between return on investment and return on life. Goal-based investing integrates both, prioritizing return on life. What good is a well-performing portfolio if it doesn't support the life you want to live?

Traditional investing typically focuses on asset performance, often starting with the "*how*"—how to select investments, optimize returns, and implement a strategy. But goal-based investing flips that around and begins with the "*why.*"

This concept aligns with Simon Sinek's philosophy: *Start with why, then what, then how.* Rather than jumping into investment products, we begin by understanding your values, goals, and financial life plan using **The FISCAL Framework:**

F – Financial Life Plan

Everything starts with your financial life plan—this is the foundation. We map out your goals, values, and life stage because investing should be built around where you are now and where you want to go. If you've already taken steps to reduce financial risks, this stage ensures your investments are structured to help support those efforts.

I – Investment Objectives

Once your financial life plan is clear, we define investment objectives for each financial bucket:

- **Short-term (liquidity and safety)** – Money you need in the near term should be secure and accessible.
- **Intermediate-term (income generation)** – Investments designed to provide stability and cash flow.
- **Long-term (growth and legacy)** – These assets can employ more growth-oriented strategies as they have longer time horizons.

Each category has a distinct time horizon, liquidity requirements, and risk parameters, all determined by your financial priorities.

S – Strategic Asset Location (Tax Diversification)

Not all investments are taxed the same way. We examine how your investments are taxed before they go in, while in, and when taken out. This helps keep your tax efficiency aligned with your investment strategy. For example:

- **Tax-free accounts** – Often appropriate for growth-oriented investments.
- **Taxable accounts** – Often used for generating current income while employing tax-efficient approaches.
- **Tax-deferred accounts** - Utilized to balance growth and income objectives.

The goal is to minimize tax implications while optimizing investment growth across various account types

C – Comprehensive Asset Allocation (Asset Class Diversification)

After determining appropriate account structures, we design an asset allocation strategy that spreads your investments across a variety of asset classes to balance risk and return:

- **Equities** - For long-term growth potential, including domestic and international stocks.
- **Fixed Income** - Bonds and other income-generating assets that help provide stability and predictable cash flow.
- **Alternative Investments** - Such as real estate, private equity, or other non-traditional assets that can further diversify your portfolio.
- **Cash and Cash Equivalents** - For liquidity, safety, and short-term needs.

This diversified approach helps reduce overall portfolio risk while ensuring each segment of your wealth is aligned with your time horizons and financial goals.

A – Analytical Product Selection (Choosing the Right Investments)

Once your goals, timelines, tax strategies, and asset allocation are defined, we turn to selecting the specific investment vehicles to help implement your plan effectively.

Examples of products we may consider include:

- **Exchange-Traded Funds (ETFs):** For efficient, low-cost exposure to targeted sectors, indexes, or asset classes.

- **Mutual Funds:** Actively or passively managed solutions to provide professional management and diversification.
- **Managed Accounts:** Professionally managed portfolios tailored to your objectives, risk tolerance, and tax considerations.
- **Separately Managed Accounts (SMAs):** Customized portfolios offering direct ownership of individual securities.
- **Individual Securities:** Stocks, bonds, or other instruments selected to meet specific goals or preferences.
- **Alternative Investments:** Such as private credit, real estate funds, or hedged strategies to complement traditional holdings.
- **Insurance or Annuity Products:** Where appropriate, to address risk management, income guarantees, or tax-deferral strategies.

These examples illustrate the range of options available. The goal is to evaluate product features—liquidity, fees, tax treatment, and risk profile—to ensure each solution has a clear purpose and fits seamlessly into your overall plan.

L – Long-Term Monitoring and Due Diligence

Investing is not a one-time event—it's an ongoing process. Life changes, goals shift, and markets evolve. That's why long-term monitoring and regular reviews are essential. We adapt as needed to keep your investments aligned with your life.

From Wealth Building to Wealth Utilization

One of the biggest transitions in financial life is moving from building wealth to utilizing wealth in retirement. Many assume that the hard part is over once they've accumulated enough money. But the truth is, the real challenge begins when you have to start spending that wealth strategically.

When you were in your 30s or 40s, investing was simple: grow your money. You had time on your side, so your primary focus was long-term gains. You may have kept some cash reserves, but the overall strategy was straightforward. Now, as you enter retirement, your financial priorities change dramatically. Instead of focusing solely on growth, you need to balance multiple objectives across the buckets we've discussed (short-term conservative investments, intermediate-term moderate investments, long-term growth-focused investments, and "beyond life" legacy goals).

After working for 30 or 40 years, you may still have 20 to 30 more years to plan for. This transition requires a fundamental shift in both mindset and investment strategy. During your working years, market volatility often represented opportunity. When the market declined, it was an opportunity to buy at a lower price. But in retirement, volatility becomes a risk factor.

If you withdraw money while the market is down, you're selling assets at reduced values, making it harder for your portfolio to recover. This is called the sequence of returns risk, one of the largest threats to retirement income sustainability. That's why incorporating downside protection strategies becomes essential. You still need growth, but you also need stability. A well-structured, goal-based investment strategy helps manage both risk and return objectives.

The Transition From Predictable Income to Investment-Dependent Income

Your income was predictable when you were working, especially for those with traditional employment arrangements. Even as a business owner, you had control over your earnings. However, in retirement, income becomes more dependent on investment performance. Some people are fortunate to have pensions or Social Security that cover their essential expenses. But for most, investments will play a substantial role in generating income.

I often compare financial independence to climbing a mountain. When you accumulate wealth, you climb the financial mountain, striving to reach the peak. But the descent is just as important—if not more so.

There's a notable story about Mount Everest expeditions. While Sir Edmund Hillary is celebrated for reaching the summit, his true achievement was even more remarkable—he was the first one to successfully make it back down. (Many climbers had reached high elevations previously, but completing the journey safely represented the true accomplishment).

In retirement, you've reached the peak of your financial independence. But descending safely—managing your wealth wisely so it lasts—is the real challenge. Without careful planning, you risk running out of money too soon or making costly mistakes. Remember, the strategies that got you here won't necessarily sustain you through retirement.

Some of The Biggest Mistakes Retirees Make—And How to Avoid Them

Retirement involves a complete reversal of how money flows. Before retirement, you were converting cash flow into assets—saving and investing to grow your net worth. In retirement, you're converting assets into cash flow, ensuring your savings support your lifestyle. Here are the common mistakes I see retirees make during this time and how to avoid them.

Mistake #1: Failing to Match Investments to Distribution Needs

Many retirees continue investing as if they're still in accumulation mode, failing to adjust their portfolios to support their spending needs. They typically make one of two mistakes:

- **One-size-fits-all approach** – They don't separate assets based on time horizons, which can lead to liquidity problems or taking unnecessary risks.
- **Poor tax planning** — After spending years focusing on tax-deferred savings, they don't strategically manage withdrawals, resulting in possible higher taxes.

The Fix:

✓ Structure your assets across short-term (liquidity), intermediate-term (income), and long-term (growth) buckets to ensure you have the right amount available at the right time.

✓ Implement a tax strategy that coordinates tax-deferred, taxable, and tax-free withdrawals to optimize after-tax income.

Mistake #2: Underestimating Tax Consequences

Many people take a "wait and see" approach, planning to deal with distributions only when they're required. But waiting until you're forced to take retirement withdrawals can backfire, forcing larger taxable distributions that might push them into higher tax brackets.

The Fix:

- ✓ Instead of deferring all withdrawals, consider strategically converting some pre-tax assets to tax-free accounts to control your tax exposure over time.
- ✓ Work with qualified professionals to plan withdrawals proactively—not reactively.

Mistake #3: Ignoring Long-Term Care Risk

Long-term care costs represent one of the biggest threats to retirement security. Health challenges can derail even the best financial plans without proper preparation.

The Fix:

- ✓ Think about ways to protect your savings from major healthcare costs, whether through specialized coverage or other financial strategies that shift this burden away from your retirement funds.
- ✓ Factor in potential healthcare costs early in your retirement planning so they don't become a financial burden later.

Mistake #4: Oversimplifying (or Overcomplicating) the Portfolio

Some retirees oversimplify by holding excessive cash and missing out on growth opportunities. Others implement overly complex strategies or don't manage risk effectively.

The Fix:

- ✓ Balance principal protection with growth potential by using a mix of investments that align with your personal risk tolerance and time horizons.
- ✓ Look at financial solutions that provide downside protection while allowing for market growth participation.

Mistake #5: Mismanaging Market Volatility

Retirees often fall into one of two extremes:

- Too much cash that loses purchasing power to inflation.
- Concentrated stock positions that create anxiety during market corrections.

The Fix:

- ✓ Set up goal-based investment categories where each part of your portfolio has a specific job—growth, income, or liquidity.
- ✓ When your portfolio is properly structured, market fluctuations become less concerning because each component is doing what it's supposed to do.

Mistake #6: "Setting and Forgetting" Without Monitoring

Retirement is an evolving phase, and financial plans must adapt to changing needs, tax laws, and market conditions. You can't set up your portfolio and assume you never need to adjust it again.

The Fix:

- ✓ Conduct regular financial reviews to reassess your portfolio allocations, tax strategies, and spending patterns.
- ✓ Adjust your investment buckets as market conditions, laws, and personal circumstances change.

Goal-Based Investing in Action

A compelling example of our FISCAL approach involves a couple approaching retirement who exited a closely held business and continued limited professional activity. They wanted their wealth to support a shift from accumulation to utilization. The situation included elevated tax exposure, potential estate-planning considerations, and meaningful philanthropic priorities. They preferred to coordinate the timing of retirement benefits and sought a strategy resilient to periods of higher inflation. Their emphasis was less on maximizing returns and more on preserving capital, improving tax efficiency, and maintaining the flexibility for work to be optional rather than required.

F — Financial Life Plan

We identified their core priorities: capital preservation, tax mitigation, supporting charitable organizations, funding educational opportunities for future generations, maintaining their lifestyle, and establishing a meaningful legacy.

I — Investment Objectives

We established purpose-driven categories for their assets:

- Liquidity reserves (near-term expenses)
- Income generation (mid-term needs)
- Growth investments (long-term appreciation)
- Legacy assets

S — Strategic Asset Location

Working with their tax and estate professionals, we implemented a charitable trust structure providing donations to their preferred organizations for a defined period, reducing their tax obligations while establishing future income streams.

C — Comprehensive Asset Allocation

We incorporated investments supporting economically disadvantaged communities while providing significant tax benefits on their business sale proceeds. We also established education funding vehicles with tax-advantaged growth potential for future generations.

A — Analytical Product Selection

We balanced preservation and growth through a thoughtful combination of income-focused solutions and diversified investment portfolios, ensuring market volatility wouldn't compromise their financial security.

L — Long-Term Monitoring

We established a regular review process to adapt their strategy as circumstances evolved. This ongoing oversight proved crucial as economic conditions, tax legislation, and personal objectives shifted. We strategically managed assets across tax-deferred, taxable, and tax-free accounts to optimize tax efficiency while incorporating insurance-based solutions for estate planning purposes.

Through our FISCAL framework, they fulfilled charitable objectives, secured reliable income streams, and established a meaningful legacy while proactively managing tax liabilities. Most importantly, they gained confidence that their wealth would sustain their desired lifestyle, ensuring their continued professional engagement remained truly discretionary—demonstrating why purpose-driven investing delivers superior outcomes compared to simply pursuing investment returns.

Fulfilling Life = The Goal. Optimizing Wealth = The Strategy

These two must work together. Goal-based investing is the bridge between fulfilling your life's purpose and optimizing your wealth to support that purpose. When properly implemented, it provides peace of mind, financial security, and the freedom to live the life you envision.

KEY TAKEAWAYS

- *What got you here won't get you there.* The strategies that helped you accumulate wealth aren't the same ones that will sustain you in retirement. Shifting from growth to wealth preservation and utilization requires both a mindset and a strategy shift.

- *Climbing the mountain is one thing—descending safely is another.* Just like climbing Mount Everest, descending is more complex than going up. You must manage risks carefully to ensure you don't "run out of oxygen" before reaching your destination.
- *Clarity drives strategy.* The first step in goal-based investing isn't security selection—it's defining your life goals. If your goals change over time (which they naturally do), your investment strategy must adjust accordingly.
- *Investing is a living, breathing process.* That's why we refer to "investing" rather than "an investment." You must regularly review, reflect, and adjust—internally (your personal goals and situation) and externally (changes in tax laws, markets, and economic conditions).
- *Defense enables offense.* With financial security, you can strategize rather than react. When you have strong risk management, you can confidently pursue opportunities without fear.

PART THREE

TAKING ACTION WITH THE RIGHT TEAM (THE "WHO" AND "HOW")

Chapter SEVEN

Orchestrating Your Professional Team

"No one can whistle a symphony. It takes a whole orchestra to play it."

- H.E. Luccock

Financial planning is a team sport. You don't have to do it alone, especially if you're already successful and your financial life is more complex. When you think about everything involved—investments, taxes, estate planning, retirement, insurance, managing debt and assets—it becomes clear that it's almost impossible for one person to master every aspect.

Building the right professional team allows you to focus more on living a fulfilling life and helps optimize your wealth without burning yourself out trying to do everything. The key is learning how to delegate intelligently.

Over the years, I've noticed that clients tend to fall into one of three roles when managing their financial lives: the **do-it-yourselfer**, the **collaborator**, or the **delegator**. Each role has pros and cons, but one consistently leads to better results.

1. The Do-It-Yourselfer

This person wants to do everything themselves. Maybe they don't have a trusted advisor, feel confident enough to manage it all, or prefer being in control. Sometimes, they're organized and proactive; other times, they underestimate the complexity of financial decisions. But here's the risk: blind spots are inevitable. No matter how smart you are, you don't know what you don't know. And the financial world evolves fast.

In my seminars, I often compare this to flying a plane solo. You might be able to get off the ground, but if you're not a trained pilot, it will be a rough flight. Or worse—you may not make it to your destination at all.

2. The Collaborator

Collaborators hire professionals, but they want to call the shots and coordinate everything. They like being in control and may already have some advisors—a planner here, a CPA there, an attorney they use now and then. Sometimes, they even step into one of the roles themselves, such as acting as their own tax advisor.

This approach can work well in many situations. But I've seen many situations where things fall apart because the team isn't coordinated. You ask your CPA about one strategy, and they say "A." Your financial advisor says "B." Your attorney says "C." Now you're stuck in the middle, unsure which way to go. It's like trying to fly a plane while listening to three different copilots give conflicting instructions. It's not a smooth journey—it's a recipe for stress and stalled decisions.

3. The Delegator

The most effective role I've seen clients take is the delegator. These people recognize the value of having a "family CFO"—a trusted lead advisor who understands their values and family dynamics and coordinates with the rest of the professional team.

I've worked with brilliant clients—former CFOs, even ex-financial advisors—who've chosen to become delegators because they understand that even the most intelligent person in the room has blind spots. They know managing a team of professionals isn't the best use of their time, energy, or talent.

A family CFO acts as your pilot while you sit back and enjoy the ride. You're still in control—you can always fire the pilot and find a better one—but you're no longer trying to fly the plane yourself. And because your financial planner or wealth manager, CPA, and attorney are collaborating under the leadership of your family CFO (often your financial planner), they're not working in silos. They coordinate strategies, share insights, and ensure every piece of your financial puzzle fits together for a smoother journey and better outcomes.

The Hidden Cost of Going It Alone

If you've been trying to manage your finances by yourself or with a loosely connected group of professionals, you're not alone. Many people fall into the trap of thinking they're saving money by avoiding advisor fees or only hiring one professional instead of a whole team.

But let me ask you this: Are you really saving, or are you just being penny-wise and pound-foolish?

I've seen too many people make costly mistakes, miss opportunities, or get frozen by confusion simply because they didn't have a coordinated strategy or a team working in harmony on their behalf.

Mistake #1: Thinking You're Saving Money

Do-it-yourselfers and partial collaborators often believe they save money by not paying professionals. And sure, on paper, it might look like you're cutting costs. But without expert guidance, you may be missing out on far greater savings or opportunities that could grow your wealth more effectively. It's like skipping a fitness coach to save money only to use the wrong technique, injure yourself, and end up paying more later for recovery and rehab.

Mistake #2: Fragmented Decision-Making

Another common mistake is making financial decisions in silos. You might manage your investments independently but not consider how they impact your taxes. Or you work with an estate attorney who has no idea how your investments are structured. When advisors aren't working together, you're in the middle trying to make sense of conflicting advice. And often, this can lead to inaction—or worse, rushed decisions made without seeing the whole picture.

Mistake #3: Underestimating Complexity

The financial world isn't static. Tax laws change, investment vehicles evolve, and new strategies emerge. I'm a professional, and I still spend hundreds of hours a year attending conferences, completing training, and staying on top of updates just to keep my expertise sharp. It's not realistic to expect someone with a different full-time career—or full-time life—to keep up with all of that. If you're not immersed in this world daily, it's easy to miss key changes that could significantly impact your planning.

Mistake #4: Emotional Decision-Making

When your own money is on the line, it's personal. Even I feel stressed sometimes when managing my own investments. That emotional closeness can lead to procrastination, rash decisions, or total avoidance, especially in volatile markets. One of the biggest values of having a trusted advisor is that they act as a buffer. They bring perspective, logic, and follow-through, even when your emotions try to take over. And because they're accountable to you, they don't procrastinate. They follow through, so you don't have to stress over every market swing.

Mistake #5: Ignoring Opportunity Cost

Even if you love managing your finances and are good at it, is that the best use of your time and energy? Time is your most precious resource. If you're a business owner, could that time be better spent growing your business? If you're involved in nonprofit work, wouldn't your energy be more impactful there? Or maybe you'd rather be with your family, enjoying life. Delegating protects your time. It frees you to focus on what brings you joy and fulfillment while still ensuring that your wealth is being handled with care.

Who Should Be on Your Team?

Think of building a well-rounded financial team like a circle. At the center is your core team—the professionals you work with regularly. Then there are others you may bring in periodically and still others who are called in only as needed. At the heart of that team are three essential players you should always have: a financial planner/ wealth advisor, a tax advisor, and an estate planning attorney/legal advisor. Each brings a distinct perspective and area of expertise.

Your Financial Planner/Wealth Advisor:

Most families have a primary care physician who knows their medical history, tracks vital signs, coordinates with specialists, and serves as the central hub for their health. In your financial life, a financial planner can play a similar role.

We serve as your financial primary care team—your planning hub. As Certified Financial Planner professionals, we are trained across the six core areas of your financial life: financial position, retirement planning, tax planning, investment management, insurance, and estate planning. That broad view helps us see more than one piece of the puzzle.

Like a good doctor, we don't address just one symptom. We help make sure your investments, tax strategy, estate plan, and insurance coverage work together. We track overall progress and often see the full arc of your life—before a business sale, through retirement, and beyond—coordinating with your spouse, heirs, and legacy.

Specialists may come and go. You might work with a business attorney while running a company, then move on after the sale; the same can be true for a retirement plan administrator or a business broker. But your financial planner can be a throughline across all of it. And it doesn't stop at retirement or estate planning: a true family financial planner supports your spouse and the next generation. We help carry your values forward, not just your wealth.

What makes this role powerful is how we connect the dots. When your CPA advises on taxes and your attorney advises on your trust, the planner helps implement those recommendations. We speak the language of each professional, translate it into clear, actionable steps, and help keep everything aligned with your larger plan.

Often, we're the ones providing other professionals with the details they need to do their jobs well. We help you live a fulfilling life while optimizing your wealth—reducing stress by coordinating your team, tracking progress, and holding you accountable in a supportive, encouraging way so you can move forward with confidence.

Your Tax Advisor: Looking Forward, Not Just Backward

Next up is your tax advisor. This might be a CPA or an enrolled agent. Tax planning is one of the six core areas of financial planning, but it's also where specialists shine. Here's an important distinction: you want a tax planner, not just a tax preparer. A preparer looks backward—they report what already happened. A planner looks forward. They help structure things today, so you're better off tomorrow. And when your financial planner and tax advisor collaborate, you get tax-smart strategies aligned with your long-term goals.

Your Estate Attorney/Legal Advisor: Protecting What You've Built

Your estate planning attorney is the third pillar of your core team. Some people work with them regularly; others check in every few years. Either way, this professional plays a big role in protecting your legacy. They draft the legal documents. They help reduce tax exposure. And the best ones go beyond the paperwork. They help ensure your plan is not just written—it's implemented, often in collaboration with your financial planner. Estate planning is too important to treat as a one-and-done process. It's an ongoing conversation.

Specialists You May Need from Time to Time

Depending on your circumstances, you might also need other professionals, including:

- **Institutional money managers** (often sourced and managed through your advisor)
- **Insurance specialists** (especially for health, business, or property coverage)
- **Business valuation experts** (a must for business owners—preferably reviewed annually)
- **Charitable giving consultants** (particularly for philanthropic families)
- **Business attorneys or succession planners**
- **M&A consultants or brokers** (especially if you're selling or restructuring your business)
- **Executive or leadership coaches**

You won't need all of these all the time. However, having a financial planner who knows when to help bring in the right person can make all the difference.

Don't Forget Your Most Important Partner

And here's one more team member people often overlook: your spouse or life partner. If you're in a relationship, your partner should be part of this journey. I've seen business owners make big decisions without involving their spouses, only to return home and face uncertainty or hesitation. That lack of communication can lead to stalled decisions or unintentional conflict.

You're on the same plane together. You both need to agree on the destination. And when that happens, your financial team can help design the smoothest flight plan to get you there.

Adult children also play a critical role in many cases, especially when named as beneficiaries or powers of attorney. When appropriate, including them in the process fosters clarity, continuity, and peace of mind for future transitions.

Creating a Rhythm for Team Communication

Your advisors may not need to communicate constantly—but timely. We all serve multiple clients, and everyone's schedule is packed, especially during peak seasons like tax time. But that doesn't mean effective communication isn't possible. It just means we need to be intentional about it.

In our practice, we always emphasize the importance of setting a natural communication rhythm among your advisors. This is how we stay proactive instead of reactive, preventing mistakes rather than cleaning them up afterward.

Annual Check-Ins and Strategic Timing

There are key moments in the year when collaboration should naturally occur. For example, your financial planner should coordinate with your tax advisor every year during tax planning season.

While advance planning is ideal, we're also ready to coordinate during busier times like tax season when timely decisions are necessary.

Another key time to review and coordinate is when we update ownership structures or beneficiary designations. If legal documents need to be updated, we bring in your estate attorney. Ideally, you revisit that legal relationship every two to five years or sooner if something significant changes.

And when bigger life events happen, like the sale or purchase of a business, a large inheritance, or the decision to start gifting assets, we'll often organize a team meeting with your attorney and CPA to ensure everyone is aligned on strategy.

Don't Wait for a Crisis

We've helped clients settle estates after a death in the family, and I can tell you—it's far easier when the team already knows each other. You don't want the first introduction between your planner, CPA, and attorney to happen *after* something has gone wrong. Your professionals should be familiar with one another well before a crisis or transition occurs.

The same goes for charitable giving. If you make regular donations, your planner should know which organizations you support and ideally coordinate with them toward year-end to ensure contributions are processed in time and in the most tax-efficient way possible.

Enable and Authorize Communication

We ask our clients to sign an information disclosure authorization form from day one. This lets us talk to your other advisors directly to move quickly, share insights, and reduce miscommunication. You're always welcome to join the conversation if that makes you uncomfortable. Some clients prefer to be present for every discussion, and that's totally fine. But giving us that formal permission helps us advocate for you more efficiently.

Share Your Goals and Values with the Whole Team

One of the most powerful things you can do is let your financial planner share your core values, family dynamics, and goals with the rest of your professional team. We often know things your other advisors don't—your behavioral tendencies, emotional decision-making patterns, or long-term vision for your legacy. When your whole team is aligned on your "why," they'll make better recommendations, and your plan will work more cohesively.

Keep It Active, Not Set-and-Forget

Finally, don't fall into the trap of thinking that once your plan is in place, it can just cruise on autopilot. Life might feel steady, but the world around you changes. Tax laws shift. Markets fluctuate. Your goals evolve. A plan that worked last year may need adjustments this year.

Your professional team must periodically check in and communicate strategically, especially during transitions. That's how we ensure your financial life is continuously optimized.

From Do-It-Yourself to Delegation

A remarkable woman demonstrated the power of letting go and trusting a team. She was smart and disciplined. For decades, she managed her portfolio on her own and did a decent job. She lived within her means, saved diligently, and stayed consistent. She didn't think she needed a financial advisor—everything looked fine on the surface.

As time passed, her priorities shifted. She wanted to travel more, enjoy her grandkids, and relax. With age came new concerns about health, the future of her wealth, and, most importantly, her son.

She knew she would never spend all the money she had accumulated. That wealth would pass to her son, yet she worried he might not manage it well. He had a history of impulsive spending, and she feared he lacked the tools and judgment to steward the legacy she'd built.

At first, she resisted engaging professionals. Managing everything herself had been a point of pride. Eventually, the risk of leaving her son unprepared felt too great. She wanted an established advisory relationship in place—one that understood the full picture and could look out for both of them.

During a comprehensive review, an issue surfaced: an inherited IRA had been handled incorrectly for years. It wasn't intentional—she simply didn't know what she didn't know—and it carried tax implications and potential penalties. That discovery became an "aha" moment.

Even with intelligence and discipline, a blind spot had existed. If something this significant was missed, what else might be? From that point, she began to appreciate the value of a coordinated team and a written plan.

Gradually, she released some control over day-to-day investment decisions. Strategies she hadn't previously used were evaluated. A tax advisor was brought in because the estate and portfolio were complex, and legal counsel joined to address planning needs.

Conversations were coordinated. A comprehensive net-worth inventory, cash-flow projections, and a written financial plan were documented and reviewed annually. The process created structure and provided greater peace of mind.

Her son was included as the household's financial picture came together. Initially hesitant, he began his own planning process and engaged more thoughtfully. Rather than transferring cash without context, she decided to cover the cost of professional guidance for him—choosing to equip him with knowledge and a framework for decision-making.

Today, she feels more confident about the path ahead. Day-to-day market watching has been replaced by periodic plan reviews. She travels, spends time at a second home, and focuses on what matters most, while the planning work continues to be monitored over time.

The reminder is simple: doing everything alone isn't always prudent. Delegating doesn't mean giving up control—it can mean gaining clarity and support, and creating space to live fully with a plan and a team aligned to long-term goals.

Footnote: This client story is based upon the experience of a client of Ameriprise Financial Services, LLC, and is unpaid. The experience described may not be representative of the experience of other clients and is not a guarantee of future performance or success. As a client of Ameriprise Financial, you may work with different financial advisors at any time.

Let Go to Grow

It is understandable to feel hesitant to trust professionals with your finances. That hesitation is often rooted in a desire to protect what you've worked hard to build. But let me offer you this: the right team doesn't take control away from you—they give you more of it. More clarity. More confidence. More freedom.

Clarity about what you want from life supports effective delegation. What do you love, and how do you want to live? What are you good at? Who do you care about? Where do you truly want to spend your time? Once you're open to delegating—or even just exploring the possibility—the next step is doing your homework.

You want people who understand your unique situation. If you're transitioning into retirement, make sure your advisor knows how to handle distribution strategies and tax implications. If you're selling a business, find someone who's helped others navigate that path. Certifications matter, but so does real-world experience. Are they lifelong learners? Do they pursue continuing education? Are they licensed and registered where they should be? You can check FINRA's BrokerCheck and other regulatory sites to verify background, history, and any red flags.

Also, consider the structure behind the person. Are they part of a stable firm? Who else supports them? What is their security protocol? In today's world, cyber protection is not optional.

Evaluate how they charge (fee-based, commission-based, or a hybrid). But more importantly, understand what you receive in exchange for those fees. A diversified compensation model may give you access to more well-rounded strategies.

Finally, ask this: Do they collaborate? Do they have a process for working with other professionals—your CPA, attorney, or charitable advisor? And do they have an ongoing rhythm for those conversations, not just a one-time handoff?

This is your life. Your team should work together in harmony to support it.

If you're already financially successful, chances are, delegation helped you get there. Whether you led a business, a team, or an organization, you didn't do it alone—and you shouldn't try to do so with your finances.

There's a kind of wisdom in admitting you don't have all the answers. That humility doesn't make you weaker—it makes you smarter. So, I invite you to reflect: Are you still trying to fly the plane yourself? Are you a do-it-yourselfer, a collaborator, or is it time to become a true delegator?

Because as life evolves, so does complexity. And as complexity grows, so does the need for an orchestrated team that works together with one clear purpose: supporting your fulfilling life while optimizing your wealth. And when you invest in that kind of team, you're not just buying expertise. You're buying peace of mind. You're buying time, energy, and freedom. You're investing in a smoother journey. One where you don't have to fly the plane—you can enjoy the view.

KEY TAKEAWAYS

- Managing your finances solo may feel like you're in control, but unseen blind spots, fragmented decisions, and missed opportunities can quietly erode your long-term success.
- The most effective approach is to step into the role of a delegator, someone who builds a coordinated, collaborative team led by a trusted advisor who understands your complete financial picture.
- Your core financial team should include a financial planner/wealth advisor, a tax advisor who looks forward, and an estate attorney/legal advisor who protects your legacy. They should all work together in rhythm.
- Delegating doesn't mean giving up control—it means gaining clarity, confidence, and the freedom to spend your time where it matters most.
- The right team is a life decision. When your professionals are aligned with your values and goals, you get peace of mind and the space to enjoy the journey.

Chapter EIGHT

Implementation Accountability

> "You are more likely to act your way into feeling than feel your way into acting."
>
> – Jerome Bruner

There's a Chinese proverb I love: "A great beginning is half of the success." That's true, but it's only half. The other half is what really counts: implementation. You can have the most thoughtful, customized financial plan in the world, aligning it perfectly with your goals and ambitions. But if you don't follow through, nothing happens.

I think of what the late Stephen Covey said: *"Everything is created twice—first mentally, then physically."* The first creation is the plan. The second creation is the implementation. And without that second step, all your best intentions and well-crafted plans go nowhere.

Over and over in my career, I've worked with clients who look very similar on paper—they have the same income, the same stage of life, and even work for the same company. I design a tailored plan for each of them, similar in some ways and unique in others, but their outcomes are drastically different.

One client is decisive, coachable, and action-oriented. They show up to every meeting, follow through on every step, and stay fully engaged. The other client might show up once or twice, then fall off the radar. They say they'll act but never quite get around to it. When I try to follow up, it's like chasing a ghost.

Fast-forward five to ten years. The first client is thriving. Their net worth has multiplied. They're retired, traveling, enjoying life, and even preparing to leave a legacy for their family. The second client is still working. They're still stressed. They're still stuck because they never changed their behavior.

Implementation is the small decisions and habits that build momentum and lead to big results. James Clear calls this the power of "atomic habits," and he's absolutely right. We've all planned a dream vacation before; you know how it goes—you watch the travel videos, read all the blogs, maybe even book the flights, and write out your itinerary. But you're not going anywhere unless you pack your bags and get on that plane. You can visualize your vacation all you want, but you won't experience it until you act. Financial planning, especially retirement and business exit planning, is no different.

Implementation isn't a one-and-done event. Once you begin executing your plan, you'll likely encounter changes, some expected, some not. The market might shift, or tax laws may change. Your priorities could evolve. You take step A, and that action reveals something new about steps B and C. Maybe A doesn't work exactly as planned. It may open the door to something even better. But you'll never know unless you start.

You don't need perfect conditions to begin. In fact, clarity often comes through motion, helping you reveal what's working and what needs adjusting. That flexibility—the ability to correct course while staying committed to your vision—is what turns a good plan into a powerful one.

Once your plan is in place, the real work begins. Our process (as a reminder, individual financial advisors have varying processes), consists of regular meetings that focus on a specific area of your plan. Every meeting includes a written summary outlining key updates, action steps, and recommendations. Before our next meeting, we check-in. We ask, "What did you complete from our last session? Did you sign the documents we discussed? Did you move forward on the items we planned?" We gently hold you accountable if something is left undone because your future depends on it. When you complete those steps, we celebrate with you. Every win matters.

We're available between meetings, not just during scheduled reviews. Life doesn't wait for quarterly reviews. If you forget something we discussed or need help understanding a concept again, we'll walk you through it. If something changes, we'll coordinate with the necessary professionals to keep you on track.

Life throws curveballs. Markets get volatile. Politics sway. Tax laws evolve. And in the face of that uncertainty, emotions can take over. When the headlines scream "crisis," don't panic. Remind yourself of your goals, your plan, and your values. Rely on your team to watch and adjust when necessary to keep you moving in the right direction. You know you are working with the right team of professionals when their core values are evident in how they show up for you:

- ★ **Work ethic and follow-through:** They are prepared and deliver on their commitments.
- ★ **Integrity and accountability:** They do what they say they'll do and take full ownership of outcomes.

- ★ **Fiduciary duty:** They put your best interests first. Always.
- ★ **Excellence in expertise:** They constantly improve their skills and bring better solutions to the table.
- ★ **Value delivery:** They anticipate your needs, communicate clearly, and aim to exceed your expectations.
- ★ **Behavioral coaching:** They help you make wise choices by anchoring your decisions in your values, not emotions.

Your Wealth Needs a Watchful Eye

Here's an example of how ongoing reviews save more than just time. A couple's financial picture changed constantly throughout the year. We caught something important because of our regular year-end check-in and a questionnaire we send to gather updates.

Their income for the year was projected to be significantly lower than usual due to losses from a few properties. That detail might seem small, but it opened up a huge opportunity. We saw that it could be appropriate to consider a Roth conversion—repositioning a portion of retirement savings from tax-deferred to Roth—to potentially take advantage of the temporarily lower tax bracket.

The timing was everything. Waiting until tax season the following year would have been too late. We contacted their CPA right away, confirmed the loss projection, obtained a recommended conversion amount, and completed the conversion before year-end.

That proactive step helped reduce their tax liability. And it was possible because we had systems in place to monitor their evolving situation, coordinate with their CPA, and act before year-end.

Too often, people think of financial planning as a one-time thing. They go through the initial process, implement a few first steps, and then disappear, sometimes for years, until something urgent comes up. That's not a plan. That's a reaction.

Here's an analogy: a financial advisory team is like your primary care doctor. You don't wait until something breaks to get checked out. You go in regularly, even when you feel fine, because that keeps you healthy.

In the financial world, it's easy to let things slide. You automate your savings, your investments are on autopilot, and it all seems to be running smoothly until one day, it's not. Inflation creeps in. Your coverage becomes outdated. Your priorities shift. And because no one's been checking in, things get missed. Implementation accountability helps ensure you're continuously optimizing. It keeps your plan current and decisions aligned, and most importantly, it keeps you on track for the life you want to live.

Footnote: This client story is based upon the experience of a client of Ameriprise Financial Services, LLC, and is unpaid. The experience described may not be representative of the experience of other clients and is not a guarantee of future performance or success. As a client of Ameriprise Financial, you may work with different financial advisors at any time.

Motivation Through Personalization and Progress

One of the biggest factors in whether someone follows through on a financial plan is whether it feels personal. If it doesn't reflect their real life, they're far less likely to stay motivated or disciplined over time. When a plan is meaningful, it's easier to commit to.

You don't have to try to do it all at once. Planning for the next 5, 20, or even 50 years of your life can feel overwhelming if you look at it as one massive undertaking. That's why we break things down into manageable milestones. Each meeting has a clear theme—protection, tax strategy, legacy, or liquidity—so you're not spinning your wheels.

A plan only becomes powerful when it's put into action. Visualization and preparation are important factors, but real progress happens in the doing. People get busy. Life gets in the way. And financial planning, by definition, is often in that "important but not urgent" category that tends to get pushed aside. But left unattended, today's "not urgent" becomes tomorrow's crisis.

Remember that implementation doesn't require you to do everything perfectly. Just focus on doing the next right thing and then the next one after that. Strive to align your behaviors with your goals and be intentional about your path. And when you slip off track, which we all do, have a strong support system to help you realign and keep going. Your investment returns are influenced far more by your behavior than by the markets themselves. The implementation process teaches you how to form good habits, correct old patterns, and make meaningful financial and life progress.

KEY TAKEAWAYS

- A well-designed financial plan only becomes powerful when implemented with intention and consistency. Without follow-through, even the best plan is just a good idea.
- Momentum comes from small, repeated actions; real results are built on habits, not occasional bursts of effort.
- Accountability and ongoing review are essential to adapt your plan as life, laws, and markets shift.

- Working with a team that embodies integrity, follow-through, and coordination helps you make smarter decisions and avoid costly mistakes.
- Personalized plans that reflect your actual life make it easier to stay motivated, take the next right step, and build lasting financial confidence.

Chapter NINE

The Cost of Inaction

"The best time to plant a tree was 20 years ago. The second-best time is now."

\- Chinese Proverb

There's a massive gap between knowledge and execution. And in that gap, opportunities vanish. Inaction is the quiet killer of progress. You might think the status quo is "fine for now," but deep down, you know it's not acceptable long-term. Still, people freeze. I once read a book—The Jolt Effect—that really helped explain this. It said that when people hesitate to act, it's not always because they're comfortable with how things are. In fact, many know they must make a change. But they still don't move because of fear. Specifically, fear of making the wrong decision. Behavioral finance calls this "loss aversion"—the idea that people feel the pain of potential loss more strongly than the excitement of potential gain.

So they delay. They wait. They tell themselves they'll deal with it after the holidays, after the promotion, after tax season, and after the kids leave home. But the more time that passes, the fewer options they have.

When Inaction Costs Everything

A couple owned real estate properties the husband had purchased years earlier at a very low cost.

As they approached retirement, they needed liquidity but also wanted to manage potential capital-gains taxes from selling. A tax advisor and a legal advisor were engaged, and a coordinated strategy was mapped out to help unlock value from the properties while potentially deferring or reducing taxes under then-current law.

But they never pulled the trigger. Maybe it felt too complex. Perhaps they couldn't bring themselves to make the first move. Whatever the reason, they didn't act.

Nearly a decade passed. When the plan was revisited, the properties still hadn't been sold. The market had dropped, and the value wasn't what it once was. Eventually, a sale occurred—but it was too late. The wife had developed breast cancer and passed away. Not only was there less wealth to support their goals, they missed the chance to enjoy the life they'd worked for. They could have traveled together. They could have created beautiful memories in her final years. Inaction closed off those possibilities.

Worse still, because of the market decline and lack of proactive implementation, what could have supported multi-generational goals became just enough to cover one spouse's needs.

If there's one takeaway from this chapter, it's this: having a plan is essential, but it's only the first step. The real change happens when you implement.

Even small steps matter. Don't let perfectionism or fear of the unknown create paralysis. Life will keep moving, whether action is taken or not. Regular check-ins and incremental moves allow you to move with it—and shape the future on purpose.

Footnote: This client story is based upon the experience of a client of Ameriprise Financial Services, LLC, and is unpaid. The experience described may not be representative of the experience of other clients and is not a guarantee of future performance or success. As a client of Ameriprise Financial, you may work with different financial advisors at any time.

Why We Procrastinate

Financial planning is inherently intangible. And because of that, it often lands in what Stephen Covey called the "Important but Not Urgent" quadrant. When something isn't urgent, it's easy to push it off until one day, it suddenly is. You've probably experienced this in other areas of life, too. Like skipping annual doctor checkups—things seem fine until they're not, and you're suddenly facing a crisis that could've been prevented. That same principle applies to your finances.

Another reason people procrastinate is discomfort. Planning your financial future forces you to confront reality, but that's not always pleasant. It can stir up fear, uncertainty, and even vulnerability. You might worry about making the wrong move or feel overwhelmed by the complexity of it all. Sometimes, people fear losing control by making a change when, in fact, staying still is what robs them of control.

Here's something I learned early on in my career. When I worked at a bank in China, a mentor once told me, "The more you do, the more likely you'll make mistakes. The less you do, the fewer mistakes. If you do nothing, you make no mistakes—so no one can blame you." But here's the problem: doing nothing is also a mistake. It's just one that creeps up on you.

I've seen so many people hold off on making a move out of fear that they'll mess something up or face regret. But the irony is that the regret they're avoiding eventually finds them anyway, only now it's compounded by missed opportunities and a lack of options.

I see another layer of delay in marriages or business partnerships: disagreement. One partner wants to take action, and the other resists. And instead of resolving the conflict, they default to doing nothing. However, that "decision by default" is still a decision and usually comes with a cost.

There's a difference between making a decision and acting on it; people often struggle with both. But indecision is particularly dangerous. Of all your resources, time is the one you can never get back. When you procrastinate, you're not just losing time—you're losing leverage.

The earlier you begin, the more options you have. Whether planning for retirement, a business exit, or leaving a legacy, starting sooner gives you room to breathe, negotiate, and design the outcome you want. But if you wait until you're in crisis mode when the pressure finally forces a decision, you're often backed into a corner with fewer, less desirable options.

Once you've made your decision, the real impact lies in how you take action. You can act from the *inside out*—driven by intrinsic motivation and guided by your values—or wait until circumstances force you to act from the *outside in*, reacting to pressures that have grown too large to ignore.

Take succession and legacy planning, for example. It's just one illustration of this dynamic. Acting from the *inside out* might mean clarifying your wishes, preparing successors, and communicating clearly while you still can. But if you delay, unexpected illness or conflict can trigger *outside in* decisions—driven not by you but by courts, taxes, or confused heirs.

The principle applies everywhere: acting from the *inside out* keeps you in control. Acting from the *outside in* means the consequences are controlling you.

When you're reactive, you're not at your best. Science shows that we lose access to our higher executive functioning under stress, meaning our brains literally don't operate the same way. You're not aligned with your ideal self, the version of you that makes wise, long-term decisions. Instead, you're stuck in the "now," trying to put out fires.

In behavioral finance, we discuss present bias, where people prioritize today's comfort over tomorrow's reward. But long-term peace of mind doesn't come from comfort today. It comes from action.

This reminds me of another saying: feel, think, do. Most people get stuck in the "feel" stage. They say, "I don't feel like doing it." Then, they overthink. They want everything mapped out perfectly before taking a single step. But successful people reverse the order. They do first. Then, they reflect and adjust. Finally, they feel better—more confident, more empowered, more in control. Instead of feel-think-do, they do-think-feel.

A Story of Delayed Action and Redemption

A senior professional had a highly successful career, earning a large salary and holding what appeared to be substantial wealth. Most of that wealth, however, was tied up in stock options from the very company where he worked.

In situations like this, familiarity and overconfidence biases can surface. When employment and a concentrated stock position depend on the same company, risk is doubled: if the firm stumbles, both the job and the portfolio can be affected at the same time.

The investor entered a comprehensive financial planning process. A structured strategy was developed to gradually diversify the concentrated stock position. A coordinated team—stock-option specialists, a tax advisor, and legal counsel—was engaged so the plan could be implemented in an organized way.

He understood the approach and agreed with it, but when it came time to act, he stalled. Life got busy, and there was no sense of urgency because the stock hadn't dropped—yet. "Let's wait a little longer," he'd say. Years passed.

Eventually, the stock did decline. Burnout and uncertainty followed, and regret set in. There's a saying: we often face either the pain of discipline or the pain of regret. In this case, there was some of both. The good news: there was still time to adjust. The plan was refined, the specialist team reconvened, and this time action was taken.

Holdings were diversified, tax implications were managed, and wealth was reallocated into more broadly diversified buckets. The investor later retired on a timeline that fit his goals and transitioned into consulting work he enjoyed.

Guidance is often available; readiness to act is what unlocks it. It's never too early to begin, and rarely too late to improve. Don't get stuck thinking, "This should have been done years ago." Taking action now is still better than waiting another year—or five, or ten.

Footnote: This client story is based upon the experience of a client of Ameriprise Financial Services, LLC, and is unpaid. The experience described may not be representative of the experience of other clients and is not a guarantee of future performance or success. As a client of Ameriprise Financial, you may work with different financial advisors at any time.

One Small Step Today Can Change Everything

Even mistakes provide value. As Nelson Mandela said, "I never lose. I either win or learn." When you take action, you gain feedback, and that feedback sharpens your clarity. You learn what's working, what's not, and where to adjust. That process builds momentum. And once momentum kicks in, things get easier. The hardest part of mountain climbing is always the first step—overcoming gravity. But after that, progress begins to compound.

Behavior change isn't instant. You won't wake up one day as the most financially disciplined person on earth. That's not how habits work. They're built slowly, consistently, one tiny adjustment at a time. Like the concept behind Atomic Habits, real change is small and steady. You stack one good habit on top of another. Eventually, those small changes create a massive impact.

Progress, not perfection, is the goal. Keep moving, keep learning, and keep adjusting. Even if you add a few drops to your financial "bucket," it all adds up. The ocean is made of drops, after all.

I've seen people afraid to spend money begin to enjoy their wealth responsibly once they have a plan. They travel more, give more, and stop second-guessing every decision because they've put a structure in place.

And for couples, the shift is often emotional too. When they finally start working together—when even a reluctant spouse gets on board—they communicate better about money and life. Decisions about vacations, lifestyle, and legacy become shared conversations instead of sources of stress.

I've worked with widows who were once afraid of finances, but because of a plan they had built with their spouse years earlier, they could take control with confidence and continue moving forward.

I've seen families more empowered to pass wealth and wisdom to the next generation. And I've seen people start to live fuller lives because they stopped delaying.

It's a beautiful transformation. But none of it happens until the first domino is pushed over. You are not behind. You are not too late. You are right on time.

KEY TAKEAWAYS

- Inaction isn't rooted in comfort—it's usually fear of making the wrong move, and that fear costs people time, money, and meaningful life experiences.
- Having a plan is only half the battle; nothing changes until you act, even if it's a small step forward.
- The longer you wait, the fewer your options. Procrastination robs you of leverage and control.
- Real progress comes from momentum, not perfection. Action leads to clarity, which builds confidence and creates a powerful feedback loop.
- It's never too early or too late to take action. One small, intentional step today can change everything.

Epilogue

"Wealth is the ability to fully experience life."
— Henry David Thoreau

Congratulations! You've taken a meaningful and often overlooked step: pausing to reflect and intentionally engage with your financial life. That decision alone sets you on a more purposeful path than many who continue making decisions reactively, without alignment or direction.

By reading this book, you've opened the door to a new way of thinking about how your money and your life connect. You've explored how the *art* of values, behaviors, and purpose meets the *science* of financial planning, structure, and strategy. Whether you're just beginning or already well along your path, this book invites you to reflect more deeply on what it means to live in FLOW — *Fulfilling Life, Optimizing Wealth.*

But insight alone doesn't lead to change. If your reflections stay on the page rather than informing your decisions, the weight of indecision and the pull of old habits may quietly return. Choosing not to act can mean delayed clarity, missed opportunities, or outcomes that don't reflect what matters most to you.

So what should you do next?

1. Email us at indigoflowwealthadvisory@ampf.com, or call us at 916-787-9988 to schedule your FLOW Clarity Call.
2. Come ready to share what's most important to you and where you'd like more clarity.
3. Use this opportunity to reflect, ask thoughtful questions, and consider whether a Strategy Session could help you move forward with more alignment and direction.

If we're a good fit to work together, you'll experience our INDIGO client experience — a planning process built around six core elements: **Individualized path, Natural rhythm, De-risking, Implementation accountability, Goal-based investing, and an Orchestrated professional team**. This is not a one-size-fits-all formula. It's an intentional, step-by-step journey designed to illuminate your priorities, clarify your vision, and implement strategies that connect your wealth with your life's deeper purpose. It's grounded, guided, and goal-aligned.

You've opened the door. Now, let's keep momentum FLOWing — with structure, reflection, and meaningful progress.

Your life. Your wealth. Your FLOW.

"The journey of a thousand miles begins with a single step."

— Lao Tzu

About Violetta Sit Terpeluk, MBA, CFP®, CEPA®, CPWA, BFA™, CRPC™

Violetta Sit Terpeluk is the owner of a nationwide financial planning franchise and founder of IndigoFlow Wealth Advisory. With over two decades of experience, she guides individuals, families, and business owners through some of life's most important financial decisions — from retirement transitions to business exits to legacy planning.

Born in mainland China and raised in Hong Kong, Violetta blends Eastern holistic thinking with Western results-driven strategy. Her approach is brought to life through the proprietary INDIGO client experience and FLOW framework — Fulfilling Life, Optimizing Wealth — which guides clients to align their financial decisions with their deepest goals, values, and priorities. Violetta holds an MBA from the Ross School of Business at the University of Michigan and began her career as a management consultant at PwC. She is a CERTIFIED FINANCIAL PLANNER™ (CFP®) and Certified Exit Planning Advisor (CEPA®), with specialized training in retirement planning, behavioral finance, private wealth management, and life planning. Her additional credentials include the CPWA®, CRPC™, BFA™, and Registered Life Planner certification. She is also a Certified Value Builder Advisor, working with business owners to strengthen and scale their companies for successful transition.

In addition to leading her advisory firm, she develops educational programs that empower business owners to grow enterprise value and prepare for exit on their own terms.

A deep believer in integrating both the art of behavior and the science of numbers, Violetta helps clients gain clarity, simplify complexity, and move forward with greater purpose and peace of mind.

She lives in Northern California with her husband and mother. Together with her two college-aged children, they continue to inspire her vision of true generational wealth.

This information is being provided only as a general source of information and is not intended to be the primary basis for investment decisions. It should not be construed as advice designed to meet the particular needs of an individual investor. Please seek the advice of a financial advisor regarding your particular financial concern.

Investment products are not insured by the FDIC, NCUA or any federal agency, are not deposits or obligations of, or guaranteed by any financial institution, and involve investment risks including possible loss of principal and fluctuation in value.

Ameriprise Financial, Inc. and its affiliates do not offer tax or legal advice. Consumers should consult with their tax advisor or attorney regarding their specific situation.

The initial consultation provides an overview of financial planning concepts. You will not receive written analysis and/or recommendations.

Certified Financial Planner Board of Standards Inc. owns the certification marks CFP®, CERTIFIED FINANCIAL PLANNER™ and CFP® certification mark (with plaque design) logo in the U.S.

Ameriprise Financial cannot guarantee future financial results. Client experiences may vary.